TRAIL
From I

MOUNTAINEERS
OUTDOOR EXPERT
series

TRAIL RUNNING:
From Novice to Master

**Kirsten Poulin, Stan Swartz,
and Christina Flaxel, M.D.**

Foreword by Mark Burnett

THE MOUNTAINEERS BOOKS

Published by
The Mountaineers Books
1001 SW Klickitat Way, Suite 201
Seattle, WA 98134

First edition, 2002

Published simultaneously in Great Britain by Cordee, 3a DeMontfort Street, Leicester, England, LE1 7HD

Manufactured in the United States of America

Project Editor: Laura Slavik
Editor: Carole Anne Peschke
Cover and Book Design: Ani Rucki
Layout: Margarite Hargrave
Illustrator: Moore Creative Designs
Photographers: Paula Petrella, Jurgen Ankenbrand, Jon Collard

Cover photograph: ©James Martin
Frontispiece: *Trail running provides a peaceful experience.* Paula Petrella.

Library of Congress Cataloging-in-Publication Data
Poulin, Kirsten.
   Trail running : from novice to master / Kirsten Poulin, Stan Swartz, and Christina Flaxel.
        p. cm.
Includes bibliographical references (p.   ) and index.
   ISBN 0-89886-840-8 (pbk.)
 1. Running. 2. Trails—Recreational use. I. Swartz, Stan, 1934- II. Flaxel, Christina. III. Title.
   GV1061 .P68 2002
   796.42'8—dc21

                                    2001007164

Contents

CHAPTER 3
Training, Conditioning, and Preparation

CHAPTER 4
Recovery

CHAPTER 5
Environmental Factors, Navigation, and Safety

CHAPTER 6
Injury Prevention and Treatment

CHAPTER 7
Bringing It to the Next Level: Ultrarunning

Dedications

K.P.: To AJ and Barrett

S.S.: To Savannah, Ben, Alex, Jillian, Jackson, and Eliza, and a lifetime of good health, fitness, and enjoyment of the great and wonderful outdoors

C.F.: To Bob Randall for his constant love and support

Acknowledgments

Many friends, co–trail runners, and acquaintances have helped us during the adventure of writing this book.

Photographer and trail runner Paula Petrella spent countless hours traveling to photo shoots in all kinds of weather and on a variety of terrain. Her easygoing and professional manner made all those otherwise long days a joy. Her enthusiasm and talents made her an integral part of this book. Jurgen Ankenbrand generously contributed his shots from running tours around the world and his valuable knowledge of ultrarunning. Larry Mercer and Jon Collard also provided much-appreciated photos.

Many members of our Santa Monica–based Trail Runners Club helped out on photo shoots, including Adam Russell, Alexis Jacobs, Amy Chan, Anders Hasselblad, Bill Timmons, Dave Carstensen, Fred Herman, Gabriel Kaplan, Gene Zhang, Gustavo DeMello, Irving Hoffman, James McCaughley, Jeff Redoutey, Kris Wong, Larry Young, Matt Armstrong, Paul Spencer, Phillip Cohen, Randy Rhodes, Rhea Hamilton, Russell Edwards, and Zhanna Drantyev. Many, including Evan Terry, offered their views on the content for this book. A special mention goes to Jim Wolff for his moral support and amusing thoughts.

Many others offered wisdom from their years of experience on the trails. Devy Reinstein, of Andes Adventures, contributed his expertise on multiday running tours. James Bandy of The Starting Line and the staff at Top to Top contributed valuable information on trail running shoes. Members of the Ultralist pitched in via direct interviews, email notes, and past posts. We would especially like to thank Ian Torrence, Kevin Setnes, Richard Shick, Peter Bakwin, and Shannon Farar-Griefer. Physical therapists Karen Mohr and Robert Forster provided valuable insight on conditioning, recovery, and maintenance.

Chapter 7, which deals with adventure racing, would not have been complete without words of wisdom from Cathy Sassin and Andy Petranek. With their helpful and gracious manner, it is no surprise that they are so successful in team sports. And our special thanks to Mark Burnett, who generously gave us experienced big-picture, inspirational adventure racing insight.

Our very special thanks to Nancy Spear and Kathryn Beaumont for their indispensable editing skills.

I would first like to thank Stan Swartz for asking me to be involved in this project. I had just retired from the business world so I could spend my time doing what I love most: trail running. At the time, I knew that an opportunity would come along in which I could explore my passion further. Four months later, that opportunity was this book.

Special thanks to the Postorino family, who inspired me to start running eight years ago. Most importantly, thanks to my husband, who makes the sun shine every day.

Kirsten Poulin

I could not have asked for a better coauthor than Kirsten Poulin. Her calm, patient, and organized manner often changed difficult and stressful moments into relaxed and productive ones. Her boundless enthusiasm and high-spirited attitude were a driving force in bringing this book to its timely completion.

I very much appreciate Cassandra Conyers of Mountaineers Books, who had enough confidence in me to ask me to write this book. Having just completed *50 Trail Runs in Southern California* with coauthors Jim Wolff and Samir Shahin, I was more ready for a vacation than for working on another book—until Kirsten Poulin came along. With her optimism and positive attitude, I quickly went into sprint mode, and off we went into the exciting world of trail running.

Thanks to Nancy Hobbs of the All American Trail Running Association (AATRA) for initially introducing me to Mountaineers Books.

My sincere appreciation and love to my daughter, Nancy Spear, for her devoted and meticulous efforts in editing this work.

My deepest and strongest appreciation goes to my generous and understanding wife, Elaine. Were it not for her support, this book would not have been written.

Stan Swartz

Thanks to Patricia Anguiano for her help with research on some of the uncommon medical problems.

Christina Flaxel, M.D.

Foreword

For the last ten years I have been at the forefront of a fast-growing movement: getting back to nature. All of us are looking for deeper meaning to life, and I believe the only way we can find it is to be explorers. Our learning about who we are comes most clearly from challenging ourselves in nature. Meaning in life is found in the great outdoors, not on a laptop, in the office, or on the telephone.

As the producer and founder of *Eco-Challenge* and the popular CBS show *Survivor,* I have witnessed how powerful nature in the raw is and how it changes people's lives. My experience as a trail runner, certified skydiver, and expedition racer has helped me understand the unique satisfaction gleaned from the great outdoors. This is why trail running is experiencing such rapid growth: It provides the joy of being in the outdoors while challenging the body. Trail running is the foundation of expedition racing in its purest form, but unlike expedition racing, it is accessible to almost everyone, from beginner to expert.

This book is the result of the authors' twenty-eight combined years of trail-running experience through dense forests, thick jungles, arid deserts, and subzero glacial and high-altitude mountain ranges, as well as the more typical mountain trails. Hundreds of articles and books were also researched, many trail runners from across the globe were interviewed. This is a very exciting and comprehensive book, combining information not available from any other single source. For the beginner, this book is a necessary tool to getting started. For the experienced athlete, it contains vital information that can provide a competitive edge. Even those looking toward adventure and expedition racing will find indispensable advice.

Mark Burnett
Executive producer of Eco-Challenge *and* Survivor

CHAPTER 1

Paula Petrella

Introduction to Trail Running

The moon lingers high in the sky, and the sun is just beginning to peek over the mountains in the distance. Each breath carries you farther along. One foot leaps in front of the other, and you carefully survey the landscape for sudden twists and turns. You are removed from the road where most athletes put in their mileage. Gone are the sidewalks, the barking dogs, the streetlights, traffic, and city noise and pollution. You have chosen a path that winds around a mountain, leading you farther and farther from the rush of life. It is here on the trail where you let go and truly run. You are alone with your thoughts, hearing only the sound of your own rhythmic breath. Behind you the bushes rustle. This sudden move-ment alerts you to look around. A rabbit crosses the trail. Taking a deep breath, you

◀◀ ▲ *Trail running can be invigorating and exciting, or peaceful and meditative.*

sweep in the scent of the dewy morning. The air is fresh and rich. You smile, knowing this moment is yours. You have reached the top of the hill. You pause, looking down into the canyon you have traversed. The ascent felt effortless. More than an hour slips by as you realize that the rest of the city is still asleep.

Trail running is invigorating, exciting, and challenging. It is often peaceful and meditative. It is a state of mind. Some of the most serene and yet physically challenging moments can occur simultaneously while trail running. This combination creates an endorphin rush unlike any other.

The desire to be closer to the planet that supports us is greater than ever. As we advance technologically, we become less connected to natural habitat. We are experi-encing an unprecedented level of comfort and satisfaction of basic needs, and the search to fulfill those basic needs is replaced by the hunt for the latest and fastest product or way to live our lives. We increase our productivity, but we lose our sense of self. We work longer hours, leaving us less time to relax. In the process, we become further separated from the environment. We hold meetings and discussions through computer terminals; we work longer hours in offices with stale, recirculated air and fluorescent lighting. We drive cars that insulate us from the sounds and smells of our surroundings. We live in areas with houses so close together that the mountains, oceans, plains, or big-sky views have all but disappeared. Once-beautiful landscapes and natural areas are being increasingly replaced with strip malls and skyscrapers.

Even when we exercise, we are feverishly cycling on a stationary bike or lifting weights in enclosed gyms, surrounded by television news, blasting radios, and lines at the drinking fountain. We watch expedition races and "reality" television shows to satisfy our desire for challenge. We long for vacation trips and weekend escapes to places where the air is clear and the sky blue, where our senses and skills are tested.

We ache for aspects of a time long ago, when humans were a part of their environment and respected the beauty and power of the land rather than living as conquerors of it. Hundreds of years ago we ran across open plains wielding spears, hunting prey for food and clothing. We ran through woods and creeks to trade for food or goods with neighboring tribes. We ran over mountain passes at times of war. Nomads traveled on foot from one area to the next to find sustainable land. We were already trail runners.

As recently as a few hundred years ago, we ran on these same surfaces. But as the roads became paved and we turned to walking on sidewalks, the surfaces on which we run changed, too. In the last few decades, runners in large numbers have headed back to the joy of off-road running.

Many of us began trail running as children. As innocent kids full of life, we ran through open fields and parks, enjoying the freedom of our own playful flight through the great outdoors. Many of us continued that joy with cross-country running or soccer in school. Others rediscovered it in later years as hikers or road runners. Leaving paved surfaces and heading for the trails has become increasingly popular. Many who have discovered trail running never return to anything less invigorating or rewarding. It is no wonder that the popularity of trail running and adventure sports grows as we attempt to maintain our most important needs: our connection to the planet that supports us and our desire to test our abilities.

The market for trail-running shoes, clothing, publications, and adventure tours further reveals the popularity of this sport. Many areas throughout the world have trail-running clubs that meet regularly to share the sport, and organized trail races can be found throughout North America and around the world.

WHY THIS BOOK?

A surge in the popularity of trail running has generated a market for this book. It will provide valuable information for road runners about to join the trail-running community and for hikers who are ready to incorporate running into their lives. If you are already enjoying running trails, use this book to improve your experience with new information and ideas. More than twenty-eight years of knowledge gained from the authors' trail-running experience has gone into this book. The years of running with groups of other trail runners have provided a wealth of experiences, stories, and information that we share.

BENEFITS OF TRAIL RUNNING

Trail running benefits not only our mental and spiritual selves but also our physical well-being. Trail running strengthens muscles in ways very different from the effects of road running. One of the more significant areas where this is true is the ankle. Running on uneven terrain develops a neurologic system known as proprioception. Essentially, it is the body's ability to respond more quickly to an outside force. When you land on uneven terrain, sensory receptors send signals to your brain, which helps the muscle groups react. As you continue trail running, you will develop increased balance and quicker reflexes. This helps prevent ankle injuries should the ankle twist while you are running.

Running down hills, much in the same way as doing speedwork, has its own benefits. The more you run down hills, the more you will increase leg turnover rate, which is the number of times per minute that the feet hit the ground. This in turn increases speed by "training" both the mind and the muscles to understand what it feels like to move the legs faster.

Running both up and down hills also strengthens the quadriceps, hamstrings, and calf muscles. Running up hills builds muscles similar to the anaerobic motion of weight training for legs. Stronger calves are able to support more body weight, allowing the ankle to maximize efficient running form.

In addition to the specific benefits listed, trail running increases general fitness, which can lead to innumerable health benefits. Some of those benefits include restful sleep, nutritional health, and optimal body composition. Physical activity helps to relieve stress and allows the body to sleep easier at night. When you run regularly, you are more likely to eat more due to an increased energy demand. As a result, you will most likely make healthy food choices because healthier food contains more nutrients. Regular trail running also increases the body's lean muscle ratio, decreasing fat and increasing lean muscle tissue.

Since trail running is a weight-bearing activity, it helps build bone strength and can guard against osteoporosis. It can also

Trail running increases balance and agility.

Paula Petrella

lower the risk of colon and breast cancer, cardiovascular disease, and diabetes. Regular physical activity lowers blood pressure, lowers blood cholesterol, and slows the resting heart rate, which reduces the risk of heart attack and strokes. It also lowers the risk of diabetes by normalizing glucose tolerance.

As if these reasons are not enough, studies have shown that regular physical activity such as trail running also increases resistance to colds and other infectious diseases, lowers incidence of anxiety and depression, helps create a strong self-image, and provides a higher quality of life in later years. But the physiological aspects are only a part of the reward.

On trails, the senses of sight, sound, and smell are heightened. These types of stimuli fill the mind and blanket out the worries of the day. Trail running can create a meditative, relaxed state, which allows the mind to calm itself from daily stresses. On the trail, the mind is able to focus on what is grand, natural, and beautiful, and is not as subject to getting caught up in the daily minutia. Trail running offers a chance for the mind to be quiet, focusing only on the sound of rhythmic breath, or on the beauty of surrounding nature. Some days the mind may wander, much the way the mind wanders in dreams. Some days you may think only of how the trail's appearance has changed from the week before, and some

RAINBOW IN THE MOUNTAINS

As we started on the trail, the night sky prevailed and the stars shone brightly. We could not see the trail underfoot, but having run it for months, we trusted the wide fire road and hoped we would land securely. The night air was damp, and the world around us slept. The only movement was our bodies, the only sound our breathing.

After a few miles, the sky began to lighten from midnight blue, and the birds began to chirp. Now above the city lights, we noticed an orange glow to the east. Soon yellow-orange rays emerged from behind the mountain. After a few more miles, the sky turned to pale yellow and the once-vivid colors gently washed out. As the sun came out, it lit the mountain range to the west, as if the switch had been thrown on a bright spotlight.

Coming down the trail a few hours later, we passed numerous hikers chatting away and bikers pedaling hard up the hill. The sun had awoken the rest of the world, and the air had turned warm and dry. The birds were actively flying about, and the plants were alive with insects.

I marveled how different it was just a few hours before and could scarcely believe it was the same trail we had come up just a few hours earlier. And I realized that a few hours from now, it would be a whole new trail again.

Kirsten Poulin

Jurgen Ankenbrand

Trail runners enjoy a magical sunrise.

days you may work on resolving issues in your life.

Ask a trail runner what they think of when they train, and you will get many answers, from absolutely nothing to fixing a problem at work, to inventing a new product, to how the sunrise or sunset looked. But in every case, trail running provides an invaluable benefit to the mind and soul.

Trail running also provides a great opportunity to understand the local geography. Running near your home can help you discover and understand the natural terrain and history of your area. If you are visiting a place for the first time, you will see so much more than what is listed in guidebooks and gain a better understanding of the land. You become intimately more familiar with the surrounding plants, animals, and terrain than you would riding on a tour bus at 35 miles per hour. You are immersed in the detail of the terrain.

The benefits of trail running help the beginner and experienced alike. If you are just beginning to get fit, trail running can make exercise pleasurable and keep you motivated to continue. If you have run road races such as the 5-kilometer, 10-kilometer, half marathon, or marathon and want to improve your times, trail running can add strength, speed, and agility. If you have run on the road and suffer from problems caused by unforgiving hard surfaces, trails allow you to keep running and ease knee problems. If you want to increase your endurance, trail running can encourage you because there is always a new view over the next hill, and time flies as your senses are stimulated. If you have mastered the marathon and want to head into the longer distances of ultrarunning and ultraracing, the place to run is on trails.

TRAIL RACING

Trail running not only provides the opportunity to experience the outdoors but also gives you a chance to test your competitive spirit through trail races. Trail races tend to be more challenging and intimate than their road counterparts. Compared with an average of 20,000 runners in a road marathon, trail races are often limited to a few hundred entrants. Because many trail races take place in national forests, through wilderness areas, or along narrow trails, race directors and public officials are careful to limit the environmental impact while still allowing people to enjoy the landscape. Because of the limited number of participants, most trail racers experience a closeness with other runners not found in street races.

The conditions, terrain, and distances of these races vary so greatly that a trail runner can always find a new adventure. There are hill climbs, snowshoe races, beach runs, nighttime races, runs over mountain passes, high-altitude runs, relay races, adventure runs, and multiday wilderness runs. The distances of trail races can be as short as 3 miles or as long as 150 miles.

Two famous races are the Marathon Des Sables, in the Sahara Desert, which covers 150 miles of sand dunes, and the Badwater Ultra, a 135-mile run from Badwater, California, the lowest point in the United States at 282 feet below sea level, to the finish at Mount Whitney Portal, at 8,360 feet.

Many trail runners schedule vacations around races in locations such as Switzerland, Italy, Malaysia, Jordan, and Morocco. There are also adventure runs, which take place in many remote parts of the world, including Peru and Patagonia. These multiday group runs cover all types of terrain, including mountain glaciers, river valleys, and remote highlands. Many trips provide the chance to run through ancient historical sites such as the Inca trail to Machu Picchu.

Whether you choose to make a great adventure of your trail running or make it part of your daily life in your local community, the benefits are innumerable.

TRANSITIONING FROM ROAD TO TRAIL RUNNING

One of the first things many new trail runners notice is a slower pace on the trails. Often new runners discover a pace 20 to 30 percent slower on trails and think they have suddenly become out of shape. Accept whatever pace feels comfortable on the trails. Realize that it is often necessary to walk during a trail run even if you would never consider it on the road. You may want to start out on trails with mild hills or terrain only 1 or 2 days per week, until your body becomes adjusted. The important thing is to listen to your body and go at a comfortable pace.

This is not the time to do speedwork. As you become more experienced on trails, you can run them more frequently, and you will find your pace gradually increasing.

Another big difference between road and trail running is the use of leg and ankle muscles. There are many drills you can perform at home or in the gym to increase balance and agility, but one of the best ways to adjust is by actually running trails.

The additional challenges of trail running will cause your muscles and heart to acclimate gradually, just as your body adjusts when you increase mileage or weights in your fitness regimen.

Mileage often is difficult to count on the trail, so you may want to go for a predetermined length of time rather than try to calculate the mileage. You can start out running for the same amount of time that you usually run on the road.

TYPES OF TRAILS

The types of trails and terrain are as numerous as the landscapes on our planet. Almost any place in which you can run where cars are not allowed, pavement is nowhere to be seen, and you are in a natural environment can be considered a trail.

Many trails designed for hiking and biking make excellent places to run. Some trails are steep and rocky, meandering

Jurgen Ankenbrand

Muddy trails provide an extra challenge.

21

through desert canyons. Others climb through lush forests, with narrow trails of soft, thick dirt covered in pine needles. Near oceans, wide and sandy beaches are great places to trail run. Many mountain ranges have wide, gently sloping fire roads, slender paths to forge, and passes to cross. In the country, open, grassy meadows or country flats with trails are spectacular places to run.

Many trails can be run through all seasons, in snow or through the heat of the summer. Some trails are in national or state parks, others are in remote wilderness areas, and still others may be in the middle of a large city park. They may be well-marked, well-traveled trails, or they may be long-forgotten paths.

HOW TO USE THIS BOOK

Whatever your goals, and whether you run for 30 minutes or 3 hours, this book is meant to inspire you and provide helpful information. It has been compiled from hundreds of resources and interviews with many experienced trail runners who, along with the authors, want to share their passion for the sport and help others enjoy trail running as much as they do.

Read through all chapters before you hit the trails. Even the experienced trail runner will benefit from new information. In Chapter 2, you will learn how to discover new places to run. You can find trails in more places than you might imagine if you know where to look. You will also learn about time and distance planning, difficulty factors, and environmental considerations. You will learn what to bring on different types of runs, including what kind of nourishment you will need and when you will need it.

Chapter 3 describes basic training principles that can help you become a better trail runner and some on-the-trail drills to practice. You will learn specific techniques for tackling challenging downhills and uphills.

Chapter 4 will teach you the importance of recovery, including how to cool down and stretch properly. You will learn how sleep patterns, massage, icing, and nutrition all work to keep you healthy and fit.

In Chapter 5, you will learn basic navigating and map-reading skills. You will learn how to stay safe on the trail, including what to do when confronted with different weather conditions, animals, and plants.

Common injuries and first aid specifically related to trail running are discussed in Chapter 6.

In Chapter 7, we explore the world of ultrarunning and adventure racing. Some of today's top adventure racers reveal the secrets of their success. You will learn inside information on training and preparing for an ultrarace and how to assist as a pacer or crew member.

Adventure, excitement, outstanding group camaraderie, incredible workouts, wonderful scenery, stress relief, and a bountiful supply of endorphins are out there, just waiting for you to put them to use. This book will help you get there.

A NOTE ABOUT SAFETY

Safety is an important concern in all outdoor activities. No book can alert you to every hazard or anticipate the limitations of every reader. The descriptions of techniques and procedures in this book are intended to provide general information. This is not a complete text on canyoneering technique. Nothing substitutes for formal instruction, routine practice, and plenty of experience. When you follow any of the procedures described here, you assume responsibility for your own safety. Use this book as a general guide to further information. Under normal conditions, excursions into the backcountry require attention to traffic, road and trail conditions, weather, terrain, the capabilities of your party, and other factors. Keeping informed on current conditions and exercising common sense are the keys to a safe, enjoyable outing.

The Mountaineers Books

CHAPTER 2

Jon Collard

Planning a Run

Imagine reaching a mountain crest at dawn just as the sun peeks over the next ridge and sprays beams of brilliant rays across the sky. You descend to the meadow in a valley surrounded by wild-blooming yellow mustard plants 6 feet high. Moments later, running through rolling hills in the sunshine, you see the city below covered in a blanket of clouds.

Now imagine running along red canyon walls at sunset in the late autumn sun. The color of the sand changes from beige to pink to red.

Imagine dashing through pine forests covered in snow. The forest opens to a quiet, mirrored lake, the mist rising from the still water. You jump across a stream surrounded by an expanse of falling leaves colored orange, red, yellow, and brown.

◀◀ ▲ *Trail running experiences change like the seasons.*

As nature and the seasons constantly change, so will your runs. No matter what the surroundings, it is just you, away from civilization, and the sound of your rhythmic breathing. This is a big component of the trail-running experience.

Planning a run can be almost as exciting as the run itself. From the metropolitan areas of Los Angeles, Chicago, or New York to the vast rural areas of Kansas and everywhere in between, miles of hidden trails traverse the country. It takes just a little exploring to discover a whole new world.

Many metropolitan areas have set aside natural parks and undeveloped areas for preservation and enjoyment. Sometimes it takes just a short drive to find oneself in the midst of wilderness. Running trails traverse beaches, meadows, rolling hills and mountains, deserts, creeks, and streams.

It is worth taking time to research your first run and make sure you have the right gear for maximum comfort and safety. A little planning will allow you to focus on the challenge and beauty of the run itself. You should be well versed on the route, distance, difficulty, trail conditions, and available water sources before you go.

In this chapter, we discuss how to plan a run and what equipment you will need. Before you hit the trails, also read Chapters 3 to 6 to learn about techniques and training, nutrition, hydration, navigation, safety, weather, plants, animals, and injury prevention and treatment.

FINDING A ROUTE

Many resources are available in your local area and on the Internet to help you find a trail. First, obtain a local map to locate state parks, national parks, and areas managed by other agencies and authorities. Contact these agencies directly; they often have detailed trail maps. Local sporting goods stores and bike shops also provide brochures, maps, and area guidebooks. Many of the trails used for hiking and mountain biking also make excellent running trails. The most detailed maps are the United States Geological Survey (USGS) topographic maps (topos). Topos, described further in Chapter 3, provide elevation contours and point-to-point distances, and often indicate whether a trail is maintained. Nonmaintained trails may be only slightly overgrown or completely unusable.

If you participate in road races, you may find a sponsoring running club with trail information. Speak with fellow runners who may know of local trails. Road Runners Club of America (RRCA) in Virginia and the All American Trail Running Association (AATRA) in Colorado Springs have lists of many running organizations throughout

Paula Petrella

Planning a course

United States; see Appendix B for contact information.

Regional trail-running guidebooks can provide all the information you will need for great trail runs. Hiking books are a good secondary resource. Useful publications and Internet sources are listed in Appendix B.

Both nature and humans affect the course of these trails. Conditions in nature are constantly changing, and maps often become outdated. Heavy rains can change the course of a trail or even wipe out entire sections. Areas can also become flooded, affected by land or rockslides or erosion, or a trail can be obscured by snowfall. Often, land managers change trails to preserve the integrity of the wilderness. For these reasons, you should obtain the most recent maps available. It is wise to check with area management agencies before your run and ask about conditions and any trail closures or route changes. If you decide to take a nonmaintained trail, be advised that you may end up doing a little extra bushwhacking along the way.

ENVIRONMENTAL CONSIDERATIONS

In selecting a route, consider the time of year and current weather conditions. Any course may provide completely different experiences in spring, summer, fall, and winter. The trickling stream you hopped over in late summer may be impassable during winter rains and snow or in the spring due to snowmelt. A dusty fire road in summer could be a mud wash in winter.

In hot weather, consider a course that provides shady areas and only moderate uphill climbs in the sun. Where possible, run near water, such as lakes, ponds, creeks, and streams. In the summer, low mountain or hilly areas and valleys can be much warmer than the city. At higher elevations, temperatures can be much colder. Temperatures can drop 3 to 5 degrees Fahrenheit for every thousand feet of elevation gain. Mountain ranges and peaks often have their own weather. A beautiful, sunny day at 1,000 feet might change to a cold, rainy storm at 4,000 feet. At high and even moderate elevations over mountain peaks, snowstorms can occur in the middle of summer. Conditions are highly changeable at higher elevations. Check with the National Weather Service or a local forecast before any run.

You should also consider weather's impact on trails. During extremely wet or muddy conditions, trails can become very fragile and are susceptible to erosion. Running off the trail to avoid puddles can damage plants and animals. Trails that are very dusty or have been recently damaged by fire are also susceptible to erosion and therefore should not be used.

DIFFICULTY AND SKILL LEVELS

Once you have chosen an area to run, consider the difficulty of the course and your current fitness and skill level. Examine elevation changes and stream or river crossings and visualize the run. Some maps provide graphic illustrations and visual images that will aid you in seeing the course before the run. Looking at an area using more than one map will give you a clearer picture of the course.

Some runs are better suited for faster running, such as moderately inclined wide fire roads, and other courses provide more adventure, such as single-track, winding trails. We go into more detail on map navigation in Chapter 5. The more familiar you are with the area, the more likely you are to find an alternative route if your scheduled route becomes impassable.

TIME AND DISTANCE PLANNING

Any trail course is much more challenging and takes longer than the same mileage run on a smooth, flat road. Even on a downhill run, you may need to slow down to jump over obstacles and make tight switchback turns. Depending on the terrain, the same

EXCUSES, EXCUSES

It had been almost a month since I ran with our Saturday morning running group. I had just completed a long run over 2 days in the Grand Canyon, and the idea of putting on my running shoes even for a short run sounded like torture. The Grand Canyon rim-to-rim-to-rim run, which included altitude gains each day of more than 6,000 feet, took almost 8 hours each day, and even two weeks later, I felt wiped out. Upon waking each day, I intended to run, but soon the day had passed, filled with excuses.

Yet in just six weeks, I was headed for Patagonia for a two-week running adventure that would cover an average of 20 miles a day through all types of terrain and weather—the most difficult adventure I had ever attempted. This realization jolted me awake one Thursday night, slightly panicked that I would not be in shape to handle the trip.

So early Saturday morning I was up and at the trailhead by 6 A.M. None of our group's cars were there. I double-checked my watch, thinking that in a sleepy stupor I had awoken at the wrong hour. Yes, it was 6 A.M., and yes, it was Saturday. Outside the wind howled and stirred up mini-tornadoes of dirt on the trail. It was unlike our group not to show up because of bad weather. I waited a few minutes and hit the trail, disappointed that I would not be able to share the experience of the Grand Canyon and catch up with friends.

After a few minutes, I realized that with no one around, I could go as slowly as I wanted. I did not even have to run the usual 14 to 16 miles we normally covered. After all, I was recovering and should really take it easy. Within a few moments, I had justified the decision to run to the old Nike Missile Station and turn around, a feasible 7.2 miles. I would be back home earlier and would have plenty of energy the rest of day. It made total sense.

A few moments later, a runner came up behind me. It was Samir, a member of our group. We chatted a few moments, speculating on where the rest of our buddies were, and headed up the trail. The sun came up over the ridge to the east. The neon orange ball of fire was surrounded by a mass of deep blue and purple clouds, as though it was peeking through a giant keyhole. We both stopped to marvel at it. Then he had to ask, "So how far do you want to go today?" I thought, "I'm already halfway there, only 4 miles to go!" and before I knew it, out of my mouth came, "How about 14 miles?" He agreed, and we were on our way.

The next 11 miles went by quickly; we talked about family, philosophy, and a host of other things that come up during long runs. Next thing I knew, we were finished! What a perfect morning it had been: the beautiful sunrise, exercising, and running with a friend who provided camaraderie and made the time fly by. It is moments like these that keep me coming back to the trails.

Kirsten Poulin

Paula Petrella

Run with a group to stay motivated.

run for a predetermined amount of time rather than for mileage. Do not attempt your longest run the first time you try a trail.

If possible, run with a partner or group. This can add to your enjoyment of trail running and keep you motivated, and it is safer than running alone. Sharing the beautiful sights, sounds, and experiences of trail running will add to your pleasure and can create wonderful camaraderie.

WATER SOURCES

Water consumption needs vary greatly from one runner to the next, depending on internal factors such as body weight and hydration before the run, and external factors such as weather conditions. You should carry more water than you think you need. (A thorough explanation of water consumption needs can be found in Chapter 4.)

You should also know what water sources, if any, are available on your route. A known water source along a route will allow you to refill and run as light as possible. One gallon of water weighs about 8.3 pounds, and the more precisely you can determine how much to carry, the more comfortable your run will be.

To find water sources on the trail, check your map and confirm with land managment officials, or check other local sources. Water is often found near campgrounds and in state park systems. Some water sources are strictly for irrigation and other land purposes and are not suited for human

distance on trails can take up to twice as long as it would on a flat road. You may need to walk through portions that are steep or overgrown, and you may want to stop occasionally to enjoy the surroundings.

For these reasons, allow extra time on the trail. If you are just beginning to experience trails, consider an out-and-back course, in which you turn around and follow the same route back. You can turn around any time you choose, and you will become more familiar with a course running it from both directions.

Because it is difficult to estimate how long any given course may take, it is best to ingestion, so make sure the water is drinkable. If your course is near a roadway, such as a beach path, scout the area first to look for drinking fountains. On longer runs, consider a portable filtration system.

WATER TREATMENT

It is a great feeling to scoop water right out of a running stream or glassy lake and drink it while on a trail run. Aside from adding to the enjoyment of being out in nature, it also reduces the amount of water you have to carry. Before you drink it, however, you must purify it so it is free of harmful little buggers that can make you sick. Disease-causing organisms in water fall into three categories: protozoa, bacteria, and viruses.

Protozoa, which range in size from 2 to 100 microns, are one-celled animals. They include *Giardia lamblia* and *Cryptosporidium.* According to Chuck Hilber, professor emeritus at Colorado State University and a parasitologist, "In one of our studies we had over 10,000 samples from streams all across America, Alaska to Arizona, and we didn't find one without *Giardia*."

It is estimated that 97 percent of all rivers and lakes in America carry *Giardia* or *Cryptosporidium*. Though the results of drinking these contaminants are not immediate, they are extremely unpleasant, involving cramps, gas, diarrhea, and bloating.

Bacteria, which are smaller, may carry diseases such as typhoid, cholera, and dysentery. Viruses are the smallest, as small as .004 microns. They are the most dangerous, because there is no treatment for viruses. Viruses include hepatitis and polio.

Guarding against these miniature invaders are two types of water treatment—filtration and purification. Filtration removes the larger protozoa, and some microfilters remove most bacteria. Most filters contain a pre-filter, which is often a coarse screen that removes the larger debris and a secondary filter that removes smaller bacteria. Filtration does not protect against viruses.

Purification removes or kills all illness-causing organisms. The classic method of purification, heating the water to a rolling boil, is effective but cumbersome due to the equipment involved. Iodine tablets, another standard purification method, are not recommended because they do not protect against some protozoa and can make the water taste unpleasant.

Fortunately, recent technologies have made water treatment more convenient for trail runners. One of the most useful systems involves a hand-held water bottle that contains a chemical purification system. To use, you fill the bottle with water. Then, as you squeeze the bottle to drink out of it, the water flows over the purifying system and comes out clean. There is also a new "Steri-Pen," which purifies via ultraviolet light. It weighs about 8 ounces and is battery-operated. To use, you dip the pen in the water. When the light goes out, the water is safe to drink. It takes less than a minute to purify 16 ounces of water. Bottled-water companies have used this method of ultraviolet-light purification for years.

See "Hydration Systems" on page 45 for suggestions on how to carry water.

EQUIPMENT

Many people are attracted to running for the simple reason that it takes little equipment and cost to get started. Compared with other sports, which can involve a great deal of equipment, technical knowledge, and expense, running is a purist's ideal.

For most runners, the only substantial investment is a good pair of running shoes. Recent technologies have also introduced clothing, navigational aids, hydration systems, and nutritional aids designed to increase your comfort and, in some cases, performance. Trail running has benefited significantly from these advances.

While running on trails you will be away from pay phones, medical care, and supermarkets, and you will need greater self-sufficiency and preparedness. Trail conditions, weather, and the length of your run determine many of your equipment needs. Personal preferences count, too: Are you a gadget junkie, or do you want only to feel the beat of the sun's rays?

FOOTWEAR

One of your most important choices is footwear. Taking good care of your feet will help keep you running for years. Whether you are trail or road running, ideally your feet should hit the ground 180 times per minute on flat areas. On trails, your feet will encounter uneven terrain, rocks, holes, water, roots, and sand. They will also be dodging various obstacles. Your shoes should hold your foot stable and provide shock absorption. Whether you choose to wear regular running shoes or specifically designed trail shoes is a matter of personal preference. However, there are important differences between a trail shoe and a road-running shoe.

The main difference is that trail shoes' soles generally have a much nubbier outsole, which provides better grip on hills and uneven terrain and protects the bottom of the foot from rocks and roots. This grip also assists tired legs in running up hills by preventing slippage. Trail shoes often have a wider outsole, which provides more stability to better handle uneven terrain, lessening the possibility of a twisted ankle.

Prior to purchasing shoes for running on the trails, you should understand how your own foot works, how shoes are made, and how you plan to use the shoe.

How Your Foot Works. The same principles that apply to regular running shoes apply to trail shoes with regard to fit. Most runners experience an inward rolling of the foot (or, less often, an outward rolling) as their feet hit the ground. This is called pronation (for outward movement, supination). This rolling movement varies according to foot type. Shoes are designed differently to compensate for the pronated and supinated runner. It is important to understand what type of foot you have so that your shoes fit well, are comfortable, and help prevent injury.

If you are not sure what type of footfall

you have, you can take a simple test. With wet, bare feet, make a footprint on a cement surface. If your foot makes contact with the cement on the outside border, heel, and ball of your foot only and not where your arch is, then you have high arches and you supinate, which means you need a cushioning shoe. If your foot makes full contact with the cement from heel to toe, including your arch, and your footprint is completely filled in, then you have flat feet and overpronate, so you need a motion control shoe. If your footprint falls in between these two, you have medium arches, are probably a mild pronator, and need a stability shoe.

In addition to footfall, there are also three basic foot shapes, and most shoe companies work from one of these specific shapes in manufacturing their products. This is why you may find that one particular brand seems to fit your feet better than others, especially in the toe box.

The American Running and Fitness Association recommends the following method to determine foot shape. "Stand on a sheet of paper and trace the outline of each foot. Draw a straight line bisecting your heel (dividing it in half), from your heel to your toes. If the line runs through your first two toes you have a straight foot. If it runs through your middle toes you have a semi-curved foot. If it runs through your last two toes you have a curved foot."

You should also determine if you land heel first or forefoot first. An examination of the wear on the outsole of your current running shoes can help you determine this.

If you land heel first, choose a shoe with good heel cushioning. If you are a forefoot striker, choose a shoe with extra forefoot cushioning.

Shoe Construction. When you are ready to purchase shoes for trail running, you should understand how shoes are constructed and what different materials are used in each part. Shoe manufacturer's claims can create a great deal of confusion, especially since each brand often uses manufacturer-specific names and technologies.

Lasts—The three-dimensional model from which shoes are made is called a "last." Lasts are either straight, semi-curved, or curved, and they relate to foot shape. Lasts are either board (or cement) or slip constructed, or a combination of both. Board lasts provide extra support and are often found in shoes for overpronators. Slip construction provides greater flexibility and is often found in shoes for either neutral pronators or supinators.

Outsole—The outsole is the bottom portion of the shoe that makes contact with surfaces and often looks like tire tread. It is glued to the bottom of the midsole. The outsole provides traction and absorbs shock. It is usually made of blown rubber, hard carbon rubber, or a combination of both. Hard carbon is more durable than blown rubber, and blown rubber is slightly lighter. If you plan to run on steep hills or where traction may be difficult, look for an outsole that has both n (convex) shaped and u (concave) shaped, or angled lugs (lugs that hit the ground at an angle)—these

Paula Petrella

Different outsoles have different tread.

shapes will help your feet to grip terrain. For rocky terrain, look for a thicker and more durable outsole.

Midsole—The midsole is located between the outsole and the upper portion of the shoe. It is important because it too provides shock absorption in addition to cushioning, and helps control excessive foot motion. The midsole is usually made up of EVA (ethylene vinyl acetate) foam and PU (polyurethane) foam. EVA is light and provides good cushioning. PU is heavier, denser, and more durable. Shoe companies may also add gels or other technologies within the midsole to provide additional and longer-lasting cushioning.

Upper—The upper portion of the shoe is just that. It holds your foot in place. Most trail running shoes are made of a synthetic fabric, which allows air to flow through to prevent your feet from getting too hot. Many uppers are also coated with a water-proofing material, which is useful if you live in a rainy climate. Shoes coated with waterproofing materials may reduce the breathability of the shoe. Look for shoes with a padded tongue to protect the foot from pressure from the shoelaces. Shoes with a padded collar (the area around the Achilles tendon) will help cushion the ankle and help prevent Achilles tendonitis.

Shoe Use and Other Purchase Factors. The next step in choosing footwear is determining your needs in a trail running shoe. While most trail shoes are made for a variety of surfaces and conditions, some have features that are best suited to a particular terrain. For example, relatively flat terrain with many stream crossings would call for a different shoe than steep, rocky, scree-type trails. Terrain and weather are two important factors, although most of us will run throughout a variety of these.

Some questions to ask yourself: How frequently will you run? If you use the shoes several days a week, you may want a pair constructed from more durable materials, or you may want to rotate between two pairs.

For what duration will you use the shoes? If you run for more than two hours at a time, consider a shoe that provides additional cushioning in the midsole and more room in the toe box. The additional cushioning will provide more protection for the soles of your feet after hours of pounding on uneven surfaces. Much like on a long hike, you would also wear a more sturdy, supportive shoe. Separate insoles can be purchased to replace the original insoles in a shoe. They provide more cushioning and protection in the heel, ball, and/or arch of the foot.

On what type of terrain will you run? Will you run through many streams or muddy areas? Select a shoe with water

Trail shoes (upper) have more traction than most running shoes (lower).

resistant or waterproof uppers. Will you run mostly in dusty, desert, or warm weather conditions? Select a shoe with optimum breathability. Are there a lot of steep hills? Look for aggressive traction on the outsoles. In general, **n**-shaped or convex lugs aid in uphill running, and **u**-shaped or concave lugs provide traction on downhills. Rocky? Look for thicker outsoles that provide protection for the feet from rocks or other sharp objects.

Do you need a hybrid shoe for both trail and road running? Many leading manufacturers make one; ask your salesperson for suggestions. There is also a "running sandal" on the market, which features quick-dry materials and an open-toe format.

Do you have or have you had overuse injuries from running? If you have experienced tendonitis, shin splints, fractures, or knee pain you may require a shoe with additional stability and shock absorption.

Trying on Shoes. When you are ready

to purchase trail running shoes, shop in the afternoon. Feet often swell and increase a full size during this time of day. Do not buy shoes because of the brand name, the color, or because your friend recommends them. Price is also not an indicator of whether a shoe will work for you. Do not buy a shoe because it is the most—or least—expensive. The most important factor is comfort.

Always try on both shoes, because feet are often not the same size. Many people have one foot that is larger than the other. You should buy shoes that best accommodate the larger foot. Try on a few types and sizes so you can compare fit. Does the sole flex easily where your foot flexes? Your heel should not slip or rub in the shoe. Try the shoes on with the socks, inserts, and orthotics you would normally wear. There should be at least a thumb's width between the end of your toe and the front of the shoe.

When buying a new pair of shoes, ask if you can take the shoes outside and run in them. Confirm that your feet stay in place and do not slide around in the shoes. Stand on a slanted surface to test the slippage factor. The shoes should support your ankles, toes, and arch. Improper shoe fit can cause black toenails, blisters, and hot spots, so make sure the shoes are comfortable when you try them on. If they do not feel right in the store, they are not going to feel right on the trail!

When you are ready to purchase shoes, look them over quickly for any obvious defects. Set the shoes on a flat surface and view them from the heel. The midline of the heel should be perpendicular to the surface. Make sure all seams are tight. Put your hand inside the shoe and feel around for any rough spots or uneven seams, especially in the toe box. These may cause blisters.

Before wearing your shoes for running, wear them for a day or two so they start conforming to your feet. Begin with shorter runs for the first week. After that, your shoes should be adequately broken in.

Lacing. Proper lacing can also aid in a correct fit. If you feel excessive pressure on the tops of your feet, use the lacing method designed by coach Arthur Lydiard: Thread the shoelace through the first holes from the outside. Bring the right lace up two holes down, and the left side one hole down. Bring the laces across into holes on the opposite sides. Repeat. When you are finished, the laces will look like parallel lines going straight across, as opposed to crisscrossing.

If your heels slip in the shoe, tighten the top laces. To prevent pinching the foot, before you lace the last two holes, thread the lace through the hole right next to it leaving a loop space on each side. Now bring the lace to the opposite side and pull it underneath the loops, then tie the shoe as usual. This will distribute the pressure over four holes, not two.

If you have sensitive spots and you need to release pressure, just skip the holes in that area.

Shoe Care. The shoe upper should be kept as clean as possible by lightly brushing off the dust, mud, or debris after each run. This will maintain breathability. If you must use water, do so sparingly and never put trail shoes in the washing machine. Doing so loosens the seams and wears out the shoe.

Running on shoes that are too worn can cause injuries, so it is important to keep track of shoe mileage. Shoes are made to last about 350–500 miles. After that, the midsole may break down and the shoes lose cushioning and support. The upper part of the shoe also stretches out, leaving the foot with less lateral support.

Replace shoes based on mileage, rather than appearance. A shoe that looks worn on the outsole may provide adequate protection, and conversely a shoe that looks new may not provide adequate shock absorption. Write the purchase date on your shoes with an indelible marker to remind you of when to get new shoes. Some trail shoes will wear out even sooner if worn repeatedly on road surfaces. By dividing 400 miles by the number of miles you run a month you can arrive at a shoe replacement date. Many people buy two pair of shoes and alternate, by wearing one of the pair only every few weeks. This way you can monitor when the support of the shoe begins to break down. Shoes also last longer when they have a chance to air out between runs.

WARM-WEATHER CLOTHING

In warm weather, your clothing should keep your skin protected from the sun's harmful ultraviolet (UV) rays and keep your body cool. The trail may be much warmer than the road, and if you are running at a higher elevation, the sun's rays are much stronger. Your body has its own cooling system, but the process uses up valuable energy. The more you aid your body's natural cooling, the more energy you will have for your run.

As you run, heat is created by food metabolism and muscle contraction. To cool itself, blood flows from the internal organs and carries water to the skin. As the sweat evaporates and cools the skin, heat from the blood is released into the air. Light, loose clothing allows air to circulate and keep skin cool, thus allowing more blood to flow to your muscles. Choose clothing that wicks moisture away from the skin, which will keep skin cooler, reducing the amount of fluid loss. Keeping moisture off the skin reduces the possibility of chaffing and blisters. Coolmax® and Supplex® are fabrics commonly used for warm-weather clothing.

Tops. The best way to avoid sunburn is to wear tops that cover as much skin as possible. According to research published in the *Skin Cancer Journal* and the *Journal of the American Academy of Dermatology,* typical summer shirts provide a Sunlight Protection Factor (SPF) of only 5 to 9. Wet cotton shirts provide even less protection. In fact, almost all wet garments lose about one-third of their ability to protect the skin from the sun.

Specially designed fabrics carry an SPF of 30 or higher. These fabrics contain colorless compounds, fluorescent brighteners, or specially treated resins that absorb UV. These clothes have a label that lists Ultraviolet Protection Factor (UPF). Just like sunscreen, the higher the number, the greater the protection. "Sun-protective" or "UV-protective" clothing caries a UPF of at least 15. According to the Skin Cancer Foundation, "Weave may be even more important than fabric type. In general, the tighter the weave or knit, the higher the SPF. Fabrics such as polyester crepe, bleached cotton, and viscose are quite transparent to UV and almost ineffective in the sun. But unbleached cotton, for example, contains pigments that act as powerful UV absorbers.

Paula Petrella

Solumbra® fabrics protect the skin from UVA and UVB rays.

To assess protection, simply hold the material up to a window or lamp and see how much light gets through. Darker clothes also generally have a higher SPF."

Even high-tech fabrics can lose some of their UPF and SPF through wear and repeated washings. For this reason, plan your runs when the sun's rays are less strong, and always wear sunscreen.

Shorts. The two most common types of running shorts are the traditional split-leg or v-notch shorts made popular by road runners, and the tighter, compression-style shorts which resemble those used in bicycling. What you wear is largely a matter of personal preference. The most important quality in a running short is that it does not chafe your skin, bunch up, or retain too much moisture.

Most running shorts contain a liner made of a cool, breathable fabric such as Coolmax® (see sidebar, page 43), which wicks away moisture. Liners prevent the need for wearing regular underwear, which may become uncomfortable when you run. The best outer fabrics are light and breathable such as polyester, nylon, or microfiber.

Shorts should provide adequate coverage so your mind is on your run, not your shorts. Most shorts have inseams ranging from 2 to 5 inches, and a key pocket in front, which is useful for carrying gel, lip balm, or any other small item you may want to access quickly.

Care of Running Clothes. Wash running clothes (sports bras, shirts, shorts) in a mild solution and do not use bleach. Allow your clothes to air dry to preserve the elasticity of the fabrics. Sports bras lose elasticity over time and should be replaced when they no longer provide sufficient support.

COLD-WEATHER CLOTHING

Some runners feel the need to remain indoors when the weather turns cold. However, this can be a wonderful time to run. The icy air rushes into your lungs and emerges in a visible gust of air. Dashing through the quietly falling snow and hearing it crunch underfoot or getting "caught" in the rain and jumping through mud puddles are pleasures that many have not experienced since childhood. With a little preparation and adjustment, winter running can be very exciting.

Wind chill is an important consideration in choosing cold-weather clothing. Table 2.1 shows the cooling effect of wind at various speeds.

You should be slightly cool before beginning a run. If you are already warm at the start of a run, you are wearing too much clothing. On your legs, you may want to

COOLING EFFECT OF THE WIND

Wind Speed Calm	TEMPERATURE (°F)									
	20	10	0	-10	-20	-25	-30	-35	-40	-45
	EQUIVALENT CHILL TEMPERATURE (°F)									
5 mph	16	6	-5	-15	-26	-31	-36	-42	-47	-52
10 mph	3	-9	-22	-34	-46	-52	-58	-64	-71	-77
15 mph	-5	-18	-31	-45	-58	-65	-72	-78	-85	-92
20 mph	-10	-24	-39	-53	-67	-74	-81	-88	-95	-103
25 mph	-15	-29	-44	-59	-74	-81	-88	-96	-103	-110
30 mph	-18	-33	-49	-64	-79	-86	-93	-101	-109	-116
35 mph	-20	-35	-52	-67	-82	-89	-97	-105	-113	-120
40 mph	-21	-37	-53	-69	-84	-92	-100	-107	-115	-123

☐ Conditions very unpleasant; thermal outer clothing necessary ☐ Skin begins to freeze if exposed to open air ☐ Outdoor travel is dangerous; skin can freeze in one minute ☐ Exposed skin is likely to freeze in less than thirty seconds

Table 2.1

Personal preference often dictates winter clothing.

wear thermal tights with wind pants on top. On the upper part of your body, wearing layers is the most efficient way to regulate temperature.

Layering. Wearing two to three light layers on your torso is the most efficient way to stay warm and dry in cold weather. It is much easier to adapt to changing weather conditions with layers, rather than with one heavy piece of clothing. See the sidebar on page 43 for information on fabric options.

The first layer, often called the "base" layer, should wick moisture away from the skin. This will prevent moisture from cooling the skin and lowering body temperature. The layer should also feel comfortable to the touch. Modern washable wool (which is very soft), polypropylene, and nylon are excellent choices to keep you warm and dry. The base layer should be worn snug against the skin, and should have flat seam construction to prevent chafing.

The second layer, called the "mid" or "thermal" layer, should provide warmth and insulation and wick moisture further away from the skin. To avoid overheating, this layer should not be too tight or heavy. Fleece is an excellent choice for a second-layer fabric.

The outer layer should protect against wind, rain, and snow, and allow perspiration to be released from the body. Outer layers are classified as water repellant, water resistant, and waterproof. Water repellant fabrics work in a light rain, but will become soaked in a downpour. Water-resistant fabrics keep you dry in moderate rain. Waterproof fabrics such as polyvinyl chloride (PVC) is completely waterproof. (Remember that yellow rain slicker and boots? That is PVC.) Unless you plan to run in torrential rains, completely waterproof outer layers are not recommended as they do not release perspiration and subject the body to overheating. The most effective outer layers are jackets made of nylon or polyester microfiber, then coated with teflon, polyurethane, or polytetrafluoroethylene (PTFE). These fabrics are "microporous." They allow bodily heat and moisture from perspiration to escape without letting in water. In rainy conditions, choose a high-quality jacket, such as one made with Gore-Tex® (see sidebar, page 43), rather than a lightweight windbreaker. Look for the following features in an outer layer:

Hood—Look for a sturdy hood that won't flop over your face in inclement weather.

Ventilation—Vents improve air circulation. Good jackets feature underarm zippered vents, mesh areas on the back or front, and mesh pockets.

Seams—Protected seams prevent moisture from getting in. Sewn seams with tape sealed over holes and flaps that cover zippers are best.

Cuffs—Cuffs should have an adjustable closure to keep water out and fit the wrists comfortably.

Lastly, you should make sure the jacket fits well not only standing still, but as you run. Mimic the motion to ensure there is ample room in the shoulders and arms, that the neck is a comfortable height, and that the jacket is not too bulky.

Many jackets contain a waterproofing finish. Normal wear and use can affect the repellency. To keep your jacket functioning well, do not use bleach or fabric softeners and use a low dryer heat. You can also use a commercial spray-on product to restore water repellency.

Running Tights. Running tights provide insulation in cool weather and keep leg muscles warm, which helps the muscles work more efficiently. Tights can also provide protection from the elements and protect the skin in case of a fall. Styles are either tight fitting or slightly loose. What you wear is a matter of personal prefer-

ence, but avoid bottoms that have a flared leg, as these can accumulate water or mud and possibly snag on a branch or root, causing a tumble.

Most tights are made of a Lycra® or spandex blend for mild weather. For colder temperatures, wear tights with denser materials, such as polartec microfleece, or with brushed fleece on the inside. Tights can be full or capri length, and other features may include ankle grippers to prevent the tights from creeping up, back leg zippers, or reflective materials.

In rainy or windy conditions, wear an outer wind pant that will allow moisture to escape while keeping the legs dry.

Other Cold-weather Equipment. In icy conditions, consider attaching lightweight running crampons or fastening $^3/_8$-inch hex-head sheet-metal screws to the outside edges of running shoes. Both provide better traction on slippery surfaces than the lugs on the bottom of running shoes. If snow is deep, consider snow-

Shoes with hex-head screws for better traction in icy conditions

FABRICS AND COATINGS USED IN HATS, GLOVES, SOCKS, AND OTHER CLOTHING

acrylic	A synthetic wicking fabric that is soft to the touch and dries quickly.
Coolmax®	A four-layer fabric designed to wick moisture away from the skin and dry quickly. Coolmax® is thin and is excellent for warm weather.
cotton	Natural fabric that holds moisture (up to 80 percent more than high-tech fabrics), becomes heavy as it gets wet (up to double weight), and loses its shape. It dries slowly and is a poor insulator. It is not recommended as a fabric for running except as a blend.
Dryline®	A combination of nylon, polyester, and spandex designed to keep moisture away from the skin and keep it dry. Good for warm weather or as a layer in cooler conditions.
Gore-Tex®	A waterproof, breathable fabric used in outerwear.
nylon	A strong, durable fabric that dries quickly.
polypropylene	A fabric that wicks moisture, has high insulating power, and helps retain body heat in cold weather.
Solumbra®	A sun-protective material that meets published medical guidelines and is based on fabric with an SPF greater than 30. It provides all-day ultraviolet A (UVA) and ultraviolet B (UVB) sun protection.
Supplex®	A soft nylon fiber that is lightweight and dries quickly.
teflon	A coating used in socks to prevent rubbing and chaffing, which can lead to blisters.
Tyvek®	A lightweight yet breathable fabric used in outerwear that feels like coated paper. It is water resistant up to an hour in moderate rain and folds into a compact size.
Windstopper®	A fabric coating that makes fabrics completely windproof. Water-repellent but not waterproof.
wool	A natural wicking fabric that retains its shape and cushioning better than most fabrics. Merino wool is a finer blend that feels softer on the skin.

shoes. See sidebar on page 44 for more winter foot care.

HATS AND GLOVES

Hats offer protection from harmful UVA and UVB rays in the summer and from rain and cold in the winter. They can also protect your head and neck from low-hanging branches.

In warm weather, caps with flaps protect your head, ears, and neck from the sun. Separate neck drapes attach to some hats

KEEPING FEET WARM AND DRY IN WINTER

- Wear wool socks with thin synthetic liners. Your feet will stay warm even if your shoes get wet.
- Wear waterproof gaiters or waterproof socks.
- Wear two pairs of socks and put a thin plastic bag between them to keep moisture out. Replace the bag if it becomes torn.
- Apply cayenne pepper to your socks. The active ingredient causes a capillary action to warm the feet. The best way to apply it is to pull down your socks until just before your toes are exposed. Sprinkle just a little bit on the inside of your socks without getting the cayenne pepper on your hands. Do not use on your feet if you have blisters or open cuts. To remove, wash your feet with cool soap and water, and then apply lotion.
- If running in dry snow, keep running shoes close to outdoor temperature before putting them on. Warm shoes will melt the snow underfoot more quickly and make the shoes wet.

to provide the same protection. Light colors will keep your head cooler, and many hats are made with breathable mesh fabrics. Some have a reflective material on the top to deflect the sun's rays.

During cold weather it is important to keep your head warm. Up to half your body heat can be lost through your head. Fleece or wool knit caps will keep you warm but do not protect against rain and wind. In heavier rain, layer with a waterproof hood. Many products include a mix of fabrics for both warmth and moisture protection.

In cool weather, glove liners will keep your hands warm, but in colder climates, wear cold-weather gloves for comfort and safety. Gloves with rubber grips on the palm are excellent for use on trails with very rough terrain. Keep your fingers warm enough so that you can turn your car or house key after your run.

GLASSES

Appropriate eyewear protects the eyes from UV light and occasionally from low-hanging branches on the trail. Trail running is not the same as running on a smooth, flat road, so look for sunglasses that stay secure when you run.

Make sure the glasses do not distort your vision. If you are running in dappled sunlight, depth perception can be difficult. Glasses with an amber or yellow tint improve contrast and depth perception, and those that carry both UVA and UVB protection are recommended.

Polarized lenses are useful for running in snow or near water because they reduce glare by blocking vertically reflected light. Some runners remove their glasses in darker areas to avoid compromising visibility, particularly if the trail surface is irregular.

HYDRATION SYSTEMS

Trail runs allow you to experience the beauties of nature and a sense of getting away from it all. But as you get away from it all, you may not find sufficient drinking water. There are two basic types of hydration systems: the harness or backpack style and the fanny pack.

Harness styles fit much like a backpack and contain a bladder with a capacity of 50 to 200 ounces. Two padded straps rest over the shoulders. Some have an adjustable sternum strap or waist strap to reduce bouncing. A small water hose rests near your chest, which makes water easily accessible. Most styles also contain separate pockets to store other necessary items. As mentioned before, 1 gallon of water (128 ounces) weighs 8.3 pounds. The harness style filled to capacity will add 5 to 9 pounds to your weight. Try it on a short run first to make sure it is comfortable.

Fanny packs are designed to fit around the hips and have pockets to hold one or

Harness-style hydration systems carry up to 200 ounces of water.

Fanny pack hydration systems

45

two water bottles, each holding 20 to 30 ounces. Additional pockets can store keys, energy bars, first-aid supplies, identification, whistle, and other equipment. Try both systems to see which you prefer.

You can also carry 20- to 30-ounce hand-held bottles. Whichever system you use, keep your water bottles or bladder clean. They can become breeding grounds for bacteria if not cared for properly. Spend a few moments after each run cleaning your hydration system. Never put one away wet. Most bladders are made of polyurethane or vinyl and can be cleaned by filling the bladder with warm water and up to a teaspoon of bleach. Let it soak overnight, then rinse well with warm water. A drying accessory can be purchased that looks like a long vertical hanger and can be used to accelerate drying.

OTHER ITEMS

A little preparation goes a long way. You will enjoy your trail run more knowing you have everything you need. Consider the following items, depending on the environment, weather conditions, and distance of a run:

Bandana—A bandana has a variety of uses. You can soak it in water and tie it around your neck in warm weather. You can put it under your hat and let it drape down over your ears and neck, protecting them from the sun. You can use it for signaling, wiping sweat from your brow, or pulling up over your nose to avoid dust and odors.

First-aid kit—Carry a small first-aid kit on any trail run. You should also have a more complete kit in your car. (See Chapter 6.)

Your first-aid kit should include bandages (varying sizes), moleskin (to prevent blisters), antibiotic ointment, a sterile needle, cleansing pads or alcohol swabs, fine tweezers, and nonprescription pain medication such as aspirin, ibuprofen, or acetaminophen.

Petroleum jelly or antichafing cream—You may experience chafing of the skin, from legs rubbing together, from a pack, or from ill-fitting shoes.

Sunscreen and lip balm—Whatever the weather, harmful rays can penetrate clothing, even if it is wet. You should protect your skin at all times with generous amounts of sunscreen with an SPF of at least 15. Reapply sunscreen every few hours if you are perspiring a lot or on very warm, sunny days. Sports sunscreens are recommended because they last longer on the skin.

Flashlight—If you begin a run in the evening or in the morning before the sun is

Some of the recommended items to carry on the trail

up, or if there is a chance you will be on the trail after dark, carry a small flashlight. You may also consider a headlamp, which is attached to the head with a comfortable elastic strap and frees up your hands.

Whistle—To alert nearby help if you are injured or lost.

Watch—A sports watch with a timer will allow you determine turnaround time on an out-and-back run or help you track your workout. Watches with an electronic compass, barometric pressure gauge, and altimeter can add to the pleasure of your run and are invaluable if you become disoriented or lost. Some watches include heart-rate monitors.

Gaiters—Gaiters fit over the ankle area of the shoe and are attached by an elastic strap to protect your feet from outside debris such as rocks and dirt. They are excellent for use in muddy, wet, and rocky conditions.

Socks—Wear socks that provide a wicking action to help keep your feet dry. A higher

Gaiters help keep out rocks, dirt, and small amounts of water.

sock provides a little more protection from low shrubbery and poisonous plants. Some socks provide cushioning in the heel, arch, or toe areas. You may want to wear a colored sock so dirt is not as apparent. Keep a pair of dry socks in your car to change into after a wet run.

Oversock—For extremely wet conditions, waterproof socks block out water while allowing the foot to breathe.

Repellent—If you are running near poison oak, sumac, or ivy, carry a skin protectant and cleansing product.

Insect repellent—Repellents containing DEET (*N,N*-diethyl-*meta*-toluamide) are most effective. However, DEET is a potent toxin and can dissolve plastics and synthetic fabics.

Bathroom tissue—Carry tissue in a plastic bag to keep it dry. Carry an additional bag to pack out used tissue; do not bury it.

Camera—Lightweight point-and-shoot models, some weighing less than 5 ounces, are available.

Venom extractor kit—If you are in an area that is known to have venomous snakes, consider this kit, especially if you are on trails that are not heavily traveled. This kit includes a venom extractor to be used immediately after a bite. It can also be used for bee or other insect bites.

Sustenance—Food, energy bars, gels, and fluids.

Navigational tools—Global positioning system (GPS), map, and compass for navigation.

Appendix C has specific suggestions for equipment for short, medium, and long runs.

SUSTENANCE ON THE RUN

WATER

Staying hydrated is especially important while trail running because there are few sources for water on the trails, and you do not want to suffer the effects of dehydration in a remote area. The body loses up to 3 liters of water per hour in warm weather during intense exercise. Dehydration losses of as little as 2 percent of body weight can impair endurance performance, and dehydration losses of as little as 5 percent of body weight can result in heat stroke.

Approximately 50 to 60 percent of a person's body weight is water. Water also makes up most of our blood volume, which delivers oxygen to the muscles and allows them to function. A well-hydrated body keeps muscles performing at their peak. Even the slightest dehydration decreases blood volume, and the body struggles to supply oxygen to muscles. Headaches, cramps, and nausea can result in addition to decreased performance.

Trail running generates body heat, about eight to ten times the amount generated at rest. Blood conducts heat to the skin, which in turn dissipates the heat. When this process is not sufficient, you perspire and

Paula Petrella

Staying hydrated on the run is essential.

are cooled off by evaporating sweat.

How Much Should You Drink? You should drink water before, during, and after any run. Exact water needs are affected by metabolism, exertion, altitude, and outside temperature. However, medical experts recommend following these general guidelines:

- Drink 16 to 24 ounces 2 hours before workout.
- Drink 8 to 16 ounces 10 minutes before workout.
- Drink 5 to 10 ounces every 15 to 20 minutes during exercise.
- Drink at least 16 ounces after exercise.

Water consumption needs generally increase in warmer temperatures and at altitude. Factors such as thirst, sweating, or urination are inaccurate ways to determine fluid intake needs. Thirst usually does not occur until dehydration of 1 to 2 percent has already set in.

In dry weather, sweat may evaporate so quickly that it goes unnoticed; in colder conditions, it may not seem to occur at all. Additionally, if sodium levels are low, the body will rid itself of water in the form of urination to prevent hyponatremia, so it is possible to be dehydrated but still produce urine.

Finally, drink cool or tepid water on the run. It is absorbed into the bloodstream faster than cold water.

NUTRITION ON THE RUN

Your body is like an automobile. It needs oil (water) to function smoothly. But your

Common trail snacks include gels, bars, hard candies, and salty items.

body also needs fuel. If you run for periods over 50 minutes, you will need to supplement your energy stores. Without doing so, you may become fatigued, dizzy, and lightheaded. Here is how your body uses and processes energy.

Carbohydrates. Simple carbohydrates, such as sucrose, glucose, and fructose, are found in fruit and candy, and complex carbohydrates, otherwise known as starches, are found in items such as potatoes and rice. When you eat, your body converts carbohydrates into sugar, or blood glucose. This form of energy is also the only fuel that the brain and central nervous system use.

Extra carbohydrates are stored in the muscles and liver as glycogen, sort of a savings account of energy. Once glycogen stores are filled, the remaining carbohydrates become fat. For the first twenty minutes of a moderate-intensity run, the body uses mostly glycogen for energy. As you run, the body begins to use less glycogen and more fat. After approximately three hours of aerobic activity, glycogen stored in the body can become depleted. Once depletion occurs, physical activity cannot continue, unless you replenish your energy stores.

The body draws glucose from the blood at the rate of about 60 grams per hour, so you should consume 40 to 60 grams per hour of carbohydrates. For example, 16 ounces of a sports drink along with either a bagel, a banana, half a baked potato, or an energy gel per hour will provide the needed fuel. The benefit of using a sports drink is that it also keeps you hydrated. The carbohydrates should be at a concentration of 6 to 10 percent. Avoid higher concentrations; they delay stomach emptying and limit the body's ability to absorb water. For example, 24 grams in an 8-ounce serving is equivalent to a 10 percent concentration. Some people experience stomach upset in concentrations of 8 percent or higher. Experiment to see what works best for you.

Particularly on hot days, you may want to dilute sports drinks slightly if they taste too sweet or syrupy. You will drink more if the beverage is palatable. Avoid any drink with high levels of fructose because it can lead to stomach upset. Take small, frequent sips at a steady rate.

If you decide to use energy gels, drink plenty of water with them. If you eat them without water, the body can pull water away from the muscles and into the stomach.

Sodium. If you plan to run for more than 4 hours, you will need to replace sodium. Sodium helps the body absorb water. Exactly how much is needed depends on the individual. Most people ingest much more sodium than the body needs, but during long periods of exercise sodium levels can fall too low and reduce the body's ability to stay hydrated. Sodium losses can be as high as 800 milligrams per hour during hot weather, but most people have enough sodium to last about 4 hours.

Sports drinks contain 60 to 275 milligrams of sodium per 20 ounces, and foods such as pretzels, crackers, or corn chips provide about 30 milligrams of sodium each. Salt tablets are not recommended because the concentration levels are too high for most people and can cause nausea and abdominal discomfort.

FUELING THE BODY AT ALTITUDE

Running at altitude can provide majestic views and a challenging workout, but it is important to understand the effects of altitude and how to minimize chances of illness and energy loss. This is especially important if you live at or near sea level and travel for a run or race that is much higher in altitude.

As you ascend to higher altitudes, lower air pressure in the atmosphere leads to less available oxygen. Less available oxygen in the air means less oxygen in the muscles, so the heart works harder to pump sufficient blood volume to the muscles. Respiratory rate increases, you breathe harder, and more water is lost through exhalation.

At 10,000 feet above sea level, there is approximately 50 percent less available oxygen. At levels as low as 4,900 feet, the body begins a process called acclimatization, in which it adapts to the change in atmosphere. Factors such as rate of ascent, altitude reached, and the time spent at altitude all affect how you feel at altitude. Age, sex, previous experience at altitude, health, and genetics also affect performance. Diet and dehydration may also change the effects of altitude. There is no way to predict in advance how you may respond to changes in elevation. Additionally, any one person may feel the effects differently each time at altitude.

Fortunately, you can take specific steps to make a run at altitude more pleasurable. If you plan to go above 10,000 feet, it is advisable to acclimate by spending a night between 5,000 and 10,000 feet above sea level. If you plan to run a trail race competitively, it takes 10 to 20 days to acclimate for optimum performance above 6,500 feet.

Proper diet can also minimize problems at altitude. A diet made up of at least 70 percent carbohydrates has been shown to reduce the symptoms of acute mountain sickness (AMS, discussed in more detail in Chapter 6). Studies show that for the first three weeks at altitude, fat is the primary source of fuel during exercise as the body tries to preserve its carbohydrate stores. This may be a safety mechanism whereby the body attempts to preserve glucose, which is derived from carbohydrates and is the only source of fuel used by the brain.

Adequate water intake is also crucial at altitude. The increased breathing rate contributes to water loss. Mountain climbers have been shown to lose up to 6 liters of water per day. To ensure proper hydration at altitude, increase fluid intake and reduce salt intake. Eat complex carbohydrates and increase your activity level gradually.

TIPS FOR STAYING HYDRATED IN WINTER
- Drink, drink, drink! Your body still needs fluids.
- Keep your hydration pack inside a layer of clothing, such as jacket or vest, to prevent freezing.
- After drinking, blow water back into the bladder to prevent the tube from freezing.
- Keep waistbelt bottles upside down to prevent the nipples from freezing.
- Add a little lemon juice to the water to lower the freezing point.

CHAPTER 3

Jon Collard

Training, Conditioning, and Preparation

Whether you are making the transition from roads to trails or you love the outdoors and want to begin running, a basic level of fitness is needed. A novice who runs 15 to 20 miles per week can enjoy the beauty and benefits of trail running on easier, flatter trails. For trail running on more challenging rugged trails, you need a higher level of fitness. Before you head to the hills, you need to achieve a basic level of aerobic fitness and understand the conditioning needs specific to running on hilly, rocky terrain.

Along with the basic off-trail training principles, this chapter discusses ways to increase your endurance and performance during trail runs. A basic level of fitness is the ability to consistently run 15 to 20 miles per week on roads or treadmills. If you are

◀◀ ▲ *Increased fitness provides opportunities for breathtaking runs.*

not at this base level of fitness and cannot easily run 5 to 6 miles at a time, you must gradually increase your mileage over a few months before starting on the trails.

You also need to be able to handle individual long runs. Long runs help you tackle the length of trails and prepare for hills. The biggest difference between road running and trail running is the hills, which are challenging on both the uphill and the downhill. So in addition to your weekly mileage totals, longer runs of 6 to 8 miles will build your endurance for easier, flat trails.

For beginners (and for experienced runners who want to increase their per-run distance), a basic training practice is to increase mileage by 10 percent per week, with alternate run and rest days. A true beginner might want to think of training in terms of time: walking 15 to 20 minutes three times a week, then walking 30 minutes three times a week, and then switching to running. Again, the key is to start slowly: running for 10 minutes, then walking for 1 to 2 minutes, then running again for 10 minutes, until you hit 30 minutes. Eventually, you will want to work up to 6 to 8 miles once a week, with shorter maintenance runs in between. If you are fit enough to run 15 to 20 miles per week, you are ready to start trail running.

TRAINING PRINCIPLES OFF THE TRAIL

Any runner—trail runner or road runner—knows that the sport demands a high level of endurance and strength. The following principles are not specific to trail running but will help you to develop a complete fitness program that will boost your aerobic ability and fitness level so that when you hit the trails, you will feel confident.

AEROBIC CAPACITY

Whether you are beginning a running program or are a more experienced runner adapting to the new challenges of trail running, you need to increase your aerobic capacity, which will allow you to run up and down trails without tiring. So it is important to understand the aerobic concepts behind a training program to see how consistent exercise increases performance.

Aerobic capacity is the ability to perform sustained, low-intensity exercise at about 70 to 75 percent of your maximum heart rate. Exercise performed at this intensity stimulates the heart and lungs to use oxygen more efficiently. This increased and more efficient use of oxygen, in turn, increases blood flow to the muscles. And the increased blood flow delivers more oxygen to the muscles, which increases the number of small capillaries in the muscles. Capillaries are the blood vessels that deliver oxygen and nutrients to the working muscle fibers. They also remove wastes produced by the muscle fibers during exercise and energy production.

An increase in aerobic capacity also increases the number and size of the cells' mitochondria. Mitochondria are the powerhouses of the muscle cells: They use oxygen to make the energy necessary for muscle contraction. This system is quite efficient. When all the pieces work together, you can sustain exercise for a longer period of time.

To increase your aerobic capacity gradually, you must exercise at about 70 to 75 percent of your maximum heart rate. The American College of Sports Medicine defines the recommended amount of exercise for developing and maintaining cardiovascular fitness in an adult as 20 to 60 minutes of continuous aerobic activity at a 60 to 90 percent maximum heart rate. Depending on your fitness goals, you will shoot to exercise in a specific target zone, somewhere within this 60 to 90 percent range. You can always vary your workout intensity; some days it could be on the light side, at 65 to 75 percent of your maximum heart rate, and some days more intense, at 80 to 85 percent of your maximum heart rate. An average of 70 to 75 percent will help increase your overall fitness level.

The most reliable way to calculate your individual target zone is to have your maximum heart rate measured in an exercise stress test. However, according to the American College of Sports Medicine you can estimate your maximum heart rate by using the formula 220 − age (in years) =

AGE	MAXIMUM HEART RATE (220 − AGE)	85 PERCENT OF MAXIMUM	65–80 PERCENT OF MAXIMUM	65 PERCENT OF MAXIMUM (RECOVERY ZONE)
20	200	170	130–160	130
25	195	166	127–156	127
30	190	162	124–152	124
35	185	157	120–148	120
40	180	153	117–144	117
45	175	149	114–140	114
50	170	145	111–136	111
55	165	140	107–132	107
60	160	136	104–128	104
65+	150	128	98–120	98

Table 3.1 This chart is based on resting heart rate of 72 for males and 80 for females.

maximum heart rate. (See Table 3.1.)

An exercise session should begin slowly. Give your body a chance to warm up for 10 minutes or so before stretching. Then, after stretching, gradually increase the intensity of exercise until you are in your target zone.

If you are a beginner, sedentary, or overweight, a recommended target zone is at a light or moderate intensity. In this zone, exercise is at an easy pace and causes only slight breathlessness and sweating. A moderate or heavy pace—the level for improving overall fitness level or training for competition—should cause obvious breathlessness and sweating. Remain in your target zone for 30 to 60 minutes and then gradually reduce the intensity of the exercise to let your heart rate fall below the target zone in a 10-minute cooldown period, followed by stretching.

TRAINING WITH CYCLES

Periodization is a training tool that allows you to train efficiently, avoid overtraining and injury, and systematically optimize your training efforts. In periodization, a training plan is broken down into blocks in which volume, intensity, and rest are manipulated to optimize performance for a targeted event or group of events. A series of workout and recovery blocks or cycles are combined to form a daily cycle, and the daily cycles are combined to form a weekly cycle. These weekly cycles are added together to form training blocks, which can vary from two- to ten-week periods. Each block ends with a taper, which is the buildup to the event for which you have

been training. These training blocks are then put together to form a yearly plan.

For example, one system is a four- to six-month plan that includes phases of endurance, strengthening, sharpening, and recovery. The endurance phase builds the cardiovascular system and increases endurance. The strengthening phase builds muscle strength to prepare the legs for the sharpening phase, which focuses on increasing speed. Finally, the recovery phase allows the body to renew itself so that the next phase is built on a strong, healthy foundation.

The endurance phase should concentrate on a gradual increase in the volume and intensity of running. Distance increases from 3 miles to 7 miles over the first few blocks, and intensity varies from light (70 to 75 percent of maximum heart rate) to moderately light (75 to 80 percent of maximum heart rate). Through the middle of this training block you will focus on increasing the amount of training, building up your distance. Typically the endurance phase lasts about two months.

The next phase is the strengthening phase, which lasts no more than four weeks. This phase is designed to increase the quadriceps, hamstring, and calf muscles and is most easily achieved by running hills once per week.

The final phase before recovery is sharpening, or speedwork. By now, the muscles are developed enough to practice running near or at anaerobic capacity, thus training the body to run faster. This phase lasts about six to eight weeks. Speedwork can be practiced on a track or by running fartleks (discussed later in this chapter) on the trail.

Within each of these major phases, there are miniphases each week. Within these larger blocks, you will reduce your weekly distance and increase intensity. This means you will move from a greater concentration on aerobic training earlier in each cycle to greater concentration on anaerobic work later in the cycle. End each longer training phase with a taper period as you get closer to the target event.

As the intensity of the training increases, you also need to increase the recovery period. With a good rest period, your body is rejuvenated and ready to get ready for peak performance again. Your recovery period can be six to twelve weeks and should consist primarily of cross-training, with emphasis on recovery running and maintenance.

REST

Rest is critical for all athletes. It is a mistake to think that more is always better or that you must train every day. During rest, the body repairs the stresses placed on it during exercise. Every run and every weight-training session stresses the muscles, joints, and bones. If such stress on the body is repetitive, the body does not have a chance to recover, which increases the chance of serious damage and injury.

The body repairs itself during the 12- to 24-hour period after a workout, which makes rest as important a part of training as anything else. You should build rest periods into your training program because they

will allow you to improve at an accelerated rate, avoid overtraining, and prevent injury. Ultimately, rest and recovery allow you to attain a higher level of fitness.

WALK WORKOUTS

Certain trails are just too steep or rocky to run, so walking is an essential part of trail running, even for seasoned trail runners. Both on and off the trail, walking also is a great way to increase mileage and reduce potential injury at the beginning of a training program.

Although walk workouts take more time to achieve the same benefits (you burn approximately 100 calories per mile whether you are running or walking, but a mile-long walk takes about as twice as long as a mile-long run), walking is much less traumatic to the body than running. When you walk, one foot is always in contact with the ground, but when you run, the entire body leaves the ground and then crashes down again with great force. Walking helps condition the muscles and joints to running because it uses the same muscles without the pounding. A common training practice for beginners or those getting back into running is to take a 1-minute walking break for every 10 minutes of running, allowing longer and easier runs.

STRENGTH AND WEIGHT TRAINING

Strength training is an essential part of a trail runner's fitness routine. Running can be particularly hard on the bones, joints, and tendons. Strength training increases bone resiliency and strength, which is extremely important for preventing injury.

When you run, each foot strikes the ground with a force several times your body weight. Strength training strengthens the muscles around the joints, which helps to stabilize the joints, bones, and tendons against the constant pounding. And as the tendons around the joints build strength, your ankles and knees will become strong enough to handle not only the pounding but also the obstacles unique to trail running, such as rocks and tree roots.

Any repetitive motion (such as running) can lead to imbalances in the body, meaning that some muscles are worked more than others. This increases your risk of injury. Strength training equals out such imbalances.

Strength training your upper body aids balance and will help you climb over obstacles such as a downed trees. Finally, strength training also enables your body to simultaneously burn fat and gain muscle.

Muscles grow stronger when you apply resistance through the range of motion in a given joint. That resistance can be your body weight, a weight machine, dumbbells, stretchable tubing, or elastic bands. For the best results, do strength training two or three times a week, with at least 48 hours between sessions to allow muscles to recover.

The resistance you choose for a given exercise should be one that allows you to perform an exercise for at least twelve repetitions, whether you are curling a dumbbell or doing leg lifts with an elastic band. Once you can easily complete twelve to fifteen repetitions, increase the amount of weight or resistance.

Trainers recommend performing one to three sets of repetitions. The majority of the benefit of this type of training is attained in the first set, but three sets provide the maximum benefit. And because most of the muscles used in running perform an eccentric contraction, in which the muscle lengthens, you should emphasize the portion of the exercise in which you are lowering the weight or resistance. In doing so, you are actively resisting the pull of gravity, and the muscle is strengthened as much as it is when you are contracting it.

Sample Weight-Training Program. A good weight-training program for beginners is 3 days a week of exercises that strengthen all the major muscle groups. Most runners do not run on the days they weight train; instead, they use these days to cross train. For example, if you weight train on Mondays, Wednesdays, and Saturdays, you might want to swim and bike on these days and confine your running workouts to Tuesdays, Thursdays, Fridays, and Sundays.

Start by doing two sets of each exercise with a first set of twelve to fifteen repetitions (or reps), followed by a second set of ten to twelve reps. After a few weeks, you can add a third set of eight to ten reps.

To choose a starting weight for each exercise, find one that challenges you while still allowing you to perform the recommended number of repetitions. In other words, you should feel fatigue in the muscle that you are working, but you shouldn't get to the point where you absolutely cannot do another repetition. When you progress to the point you can easily lift the maximum number of weights for a set, you'll want to increase the load.

There are a few ways to structure your weight-training sessions. A "split routine" focuses on one muscle group at a time. For example, on Mondays you might target the upper body and on Wednesdays, the lower body. Or, you can do a strength-training workout that allows you to work your overall body on each day you train, choosing one exercise for each major body part.

Another approach is to do a "circuit" weight routine, performing one set of each exercise and then starting again at the beginning for a second set. (Basically, you work your whole body once, and then do it again. For some people, this is a faster way of getting through the workout.)

Whichever workout you choose, start each session with a 10-minute warm-up and end it with a cool down and a stretching session. See specific exercise suggestions below.

WEIGHT EXERCISES FOR EACH MUSCLE GROUP

Lower Body
Hips: hip abductor using the weight machine

Quadriceps: leg press, leg extensions, and squats (holding dumbbells at your side, stand with your feet hip width apart; slowly squat, stopping well before your thighs are parallel to the ground; rise up and repeat)

Hamstrings: lying leg curls, seated leg curls, standing leg curls

Calves: calf raises, with or without weights

Shins: toe taps (tap your toes as quickly as you can for 30–45 seconds, concentrating on the movement between the shin and the ankle; you can do this standing or even seated at your desk); pulley pulls (using a weighted stack with a pulley handle, place the handle over the top of the foot and move your toes up and down—like a toe tap—which will contract the shin)

Abdominals
All-over abdominals: sit-ups either on a machine with weights or with a resistance ball

Lower abdominals: reverse sit-ups

To get in the best possible shape for trail running, equally strengthen the lower body, the abdominals, the chest and back, and the arms and shoulders. The lower body—specifically the hip extensors, hip flexors, quadriceps, hamstrings, calf muscles, shins, and outside ankle muscles—bears most of the load while running. (Because it takes between 12 to 24 hours for the muscles to recover from a strength-training workout, many runners do not weight train for 4 to 7 days leading up to a race or a long run.)

Targeting the upper body—the abdominals, chest and back, and arms and shoulders—help runners balance their bodies and keep good running form. Strong abdominals help not only with balance but also with maintaining form up and down hills. A developed chest and back are essential for balance, and strong arms and shoulders help especially with downhill speed.

STRETCHING AND FLEXIBILITY

Flexibility is an important part of conditioning because it prevents injury and translates

Chest and Back

Chest: bench press, barbell bench press, dumbbell press (similar to a bench press, except you hold a dumbbell in each hand. This offers more consistent resistance than a barbell, which prevents your shoulders from rotating inward. Dumbbell flies are not recommended because the weight is heaviest when your arms are in their weakest position.)

Back: wide grip pull-ups and assisted pull-ups with a Gravitron machine, seated rows, lat pull-downs (grip the bar so that your hands are shoulder-width apart and your palms are facing you; if you hold the bar with too wide of a grip, your biceps tire more quickly than your back, and this stresses your rotator-cuff muscles.)

Back extensions (to be done with abdominals to work the opposing muscles): with a resistance ball or on a machine

Arms and Shoulders

Shoulders: dumbbell presses, machine shoulder presses

Triceps: dumbbell kickbacks, pulley kickbacks, pulley pull-downs

Biceps: standing barbell curls, seated dumbbell curls (perform in a seated position on an incline board with the back adjusted to a 45-degree angle; this angle allows the bench to support your lower back and creates a more effective and complete muscle contraction)

into better running posture on the trails. This leads to more efficient and stronger running.

Overall flexibility consists of preworkout and postworkout stretching, which is called static stretching, but it also includes some serious active stretching. Static stretching lengthens the belly of the muscle to keep it from tightening and pulling. Active stretching improves overall flexibility.

Prerun stretching should be done after a 10-minute warmup because stretching a cold muscle can strain or even tear it. For trail running, focus your stretching on the legs, hips, and ankles. Chapter 4 includes a thorough description of prerun and postrun stretches.

What many runners do not know is that increasing overall flexibility takes more than just prerun and postrun stretching. This kind of static stretching is an extremely important part of a preworkout and postworkout routine, but it will not necessarily help you overcome a runner's notorious inflexibility (especially in the hamstrings and hips). Just as you might weight train two or three times a week, adding one to two sessions of flexibility training or active stretching a week to your training program increases your overall range of motion.

Flexibility Training. Pilates and yoga are two examples of flexibility training. Pilates is a series of stretching and strengthening exercises originally developed for ballet dancers to tone and lengthen their muscles. It has become quite popular, and classes are offered in many gyms. You can do Pilates in mat Pilates classes, where all the exercises are done on the floor in a group, or you can use Pilates equipment—contraptions called reformers, which use resistance to help lengthen the muscles. To do this you usually need to work with a trainer in one-on-one sessions.

Yoga is another effective way to increase flexibility. Yoga classes are offered at most gyms, YMCAs, and yoga studios. You can learn the poses quickly and correctly in a class, but you can also practice yoga at home with a video or book.

Active Stretching. Active stretching involves movement through the stretches, and because you can also use some resistance in this kind of stretching (holding light dumbbells, for example), your muscles are both lengthened and strengthened.

Standing ankle extension—Lean into a wall with hands at shoulder height with your feet 2 feet away from the wall, flat on the floor. In this position, you'll feel the stretch at the backs of your ankles. Hold this for several seconds and then rise up on the balls of your feet. You'll feel this stretch now in a slightly different area. Hold this for several seconds, lower, and repeat for two to three sets.

Squat stretch—This is a great warm-up exercise for the muscles used around the knees in running. Stand with your feet hips-width apart, feet flat, and trunk erect, with a slightly arched lower back. Keep your back in this slightly arched position as you slowly squat, stopping well before your

YOGA

For eight years, running was the only way I exercised. Those eight years included training for and running in the Boston Marathon, treadmill workouts during dreary Northeastern winters, and trail running in the wilds of Idaho.

About a year ago I began to notice that I did not recover from my runs quite as well anymore. I was stiff for a good 15 minutes at the beginning of a run, and sometimes my right knee was sore for several days after a long run, and then it began to be sore after every run. I knew that to keep running, I'd have to adjust my attitude toward the sport.

Although I was still young, I was no longer young enough to just go out for a run without considering the effects—the pulls, tears, and overall soreness—it would have on my body. I decided to start taking care of my whole body (giving my legs, knees, feet, and ankles a break from the constant pounding), and I started doing yoga.

I knew that practicing yoga would have positive physical effects, but at first the poses and stretching were anathema to a body used to running 25 to 30 miles a week. My tight hamstrings limited my ability to do any of the forward bends; my tight hips limited my ability to do just about everything else. But I kept at it and started doing yoga two or three times a week.

Slowly, week by week, month by month, my flexibility increased. Yoga postures required me to use my entire body: shoulders, neck, back, abdomen, triceps, and wrists, as well as the muscles I was used to using in my legs. But I started using them all in a different way, strengthening, stretching, and toning. My body became more balanced.

Slowly, my hands began to get closer to the floor in forward bends. In the downward-dog pose—a very basic forward bend that stretches both the hamstrings and the back—I felt my hamstrings lengthen enough for my heels to finally touch the ground.

Now I practice yoga as many times a week as I run, and it has complemented my running. I feel stronger and more balanced on the trails. Often, I do a few yoga poses as a cooldown after a run. More importantly, perhaps, I find that my running has taken on a less competitive and more meditative quality. As one gets further into a yoga practice, breathing becomes as important as alignment in the poses, and I can take this breathing work with me on the trail. I do not worry as much about how fast and far I am going: The act of being on the trail and enjoying the sweat, the challenge, and the outdoors is as important as burning calories and working out.

Did I mention I can bend over and touch the floor for the first time in eight years?

Kathryn Beaumont

thighs are parallel to the ground. Rise up and repeat with an up "one-two" count and a down "one-two" count.

Lunge—This stretch warms up the hip flexors. Begin with your feet hips-width apart. Take a very long step forward, planting one foot with the toes forward. Keep the rear leg straight but relaxed; the front leg should support your weight. Hold for a count of two and push back to standing. Repeat with the other leg, using a forward "one-two" count and then a back "one-two" count.

CROSS-TRAINING

Cross-training is the use of another sport to give the legs and feet a respite from the constant pounding of running. Incorporating a new sport into a training routine protects against injury by strengthening more muscle groups than does running alone. Wise runners use it as a supplement to running, and when they are injured, they use it as a substitute; however, the best time to start cross-training is when you are free from injury so you will not have to start an entirely new sport while injured. To work a new sport into your usual training program, replace a shorter run with cross-training, or cross-train instead of resting. The following are some cross-training exercises that complement running.

Biking. Biking is an excellent cardiovascular and muscular workout that places almost no impact stress on the feet and legs. If you use a stationary bike, a heart monitor will help keep your heart rate in your target range for 30 to 60 minutes. To minimize the strain on feet and legs and to maximize the cardiovascular effects of a stationary bike, it is best to pedal at 100 or more rotations per minute in an easy gear.

Of course, road bikes or mountain bikes are another option. They actually get you outdoors and offer the opportunity to train with a local group or club.

Swimming. Swimming works your legs and your upper body with no impact, and it might be the best overall conditioning exercise. Swimming uses almost every large muscle group in the legs, arms, and trunk, and it provides a cardiovascular workout as well.

You can also run in the shallow end of a pool, which results in almost no impact on your legs or feet. If you buy a flotation belt to hook to the side of the pool, you can run suspended in place (this is called aqua-running). Joining a swim class at your local pool will increase your cardiovascular proficiency in the water and develop your swimming skills.

Spinning. Spinning classes are now almost ubiquitous in gyms and provide an alternative to high-impact aerobic exercise. Spinning is very different from riding a bicycle or using a stationary bike. As an instructor-led group exercise, participants usually find themselves pedalling faster and getting more of a cardiovascular workout than if they were biking on a trail or doing a timed workout on a stationary bike. The best part about spinning is that with exciting music and an enthusiastic instructor you can push your endurance to a new level.

In-Line Skating. In-line skating uses many of the same muscle groups as cross-country skiing and running. Although the muscle actions of in-line skating are similar to running, there is minimal impact on the muscles, and you can go much faster. The hardest part of learning to skate is keeping your balance (helmets, knee and elbow pads, and wrist guards are essential). Mastering balance will help you on the trail as well.

Treadmill Work. The treadmill is a good off-trail resource for runners. Because a treadmill's surface is more flexible than the road surface, it is less stressful on legs, feet, and joints. Another benefit of treadmills is that you can adjust the elevation and pace to meet specific training goals. You can do hill training and speedwork and design fartlek interval workouts to boost your aerobic and anaerobic capacity. "Fartlek" is the Swedish word for "interval." As it applies to training, a fartlek is a specific method of running in which several speed pickups are incorporated into a regular distance run. Fartleks can be done during any run—on roads and trails—but on the treadmill, they give you a challenging workout, provide direct feedback as to how well you are doing and how far you have gone, and combat the boredom sometimes associated with the treadmill. For example, a treadmill fartlek session might be to start running at your base or recovery pace (if you are an experienced runner, this might be your marathon or 10-kilometer pace, to which you would add 30 seconds per mile) for 0.1 mile. Increase the speed 5 seconds per mile for the next 0.1 mile, and then drop back to your starting pace for 0.1 mile. You would increase your speed a little more for the next 0.1 mile, and so on, maybe even throwing in a little hill work. Even if a treadmill at the gym is the only running you can do during a busy week, total mileage combined with fartlek sessions can still get you trail-ready for the weekend.

TRACK WORKOUTS

Use track workouts in your training to increase your speed. Before you jump into track workouts, however, make sure you have spent adequate time developing a solid training base in preparation for this faster, high-intensity training. The body must be strong enough to handle the additional stress that speedwork on the track can place on your joints and your cardiovascular system. Track sessions teach your body to handle a fast pace for a short period of time and to accept some mild discomfort, which is necessary for optimum performance. You develop the ability to run fast while staying relaxed.

Track workouts are effective because they improve not only the heart's capacity to deliver oxygen to the muscles but also the muscles' ability to use that oxygen to clear lactate (lactic acid) from the blood (lactate is a byproduct of cellular metabolism). The result is that you elevate your lactate threshold, which allows you to run faster.

Once a week, use these workouts to run a bit faster than your projected best race pace. For example, you can try 2-minute surges at a pace a little faster than your 5-kilometer pace, followed by a 1-minute recovery jog. Start with one or two surges per workout and work up to twelve.

You need not go to a track to do these workouts; you can also do them on the road or on the trail. But if you have a track to use, you have a couple of surge and recovery options: 800-meter runs with 400-meter recovery jogs , 400-meter runs with 200-meter recovery segments, or even 200-meter runs with 100-meter recovery segments.

Because your goal is consistent times, you should aim to make each of your surge sections last the same amount of time plus or minus 5 seconds. Over time, you can work toward cutting down the rest interval rather than increasing the speed of each interval; this replicates the physical and psychological stress of a run or race, during which you have no recovery period. Furthermore, these surges of speed and energy can help propel you up the last hill on the trail.

WORKOUTS ON THE TRAIL

Once you reach a level of fitness that allows you to hit the trails with some level of comfort, you can use your trail runs themselves to improve your fitness and performance.

INTERVALS

The theory behind track workouts can be carried to the trail as well. Unless you are doing hill repeats, it is a good idea to practice your speedwork on a flat trail. Try running at a slightly faster pace than your 5-kilometer pace for 3 minutes, followed by a 2-minute recovery period. As with track workouts, start with one or two surges and try to work up to twelve surges, and do such speedwork only once a week.

HILL WORK AND REPEATS

Hill workouts build muscular and cardiovascular strength and prepare you for faster track workouts. The hill you use can be either a road or part of a trail; try to find one with a 4 to 6 percent grade that will take about 90 seconds to run.

Because hill work is more difficult and uses different muscles than running on a flat surface, you should sandwich these workouts between a 20-minute warm-up and a 20-minute cooldown to avoid straining or pulling a muscle.

Run uphill for 90 seconds at the effort you might use for a 1-hour run. You should be breathless by the time you hit 90 seconds. When you have run for 90 seconds, notice where you are and jog back down the hill to where you started. Turn around and repeat the uphill run five times. If you started out at a reasonable pace, you should be able to get to the same spot—or farther—in 90 seconds on all six runs. If you cannot get to the original spot, start slower the next time you go out for hill work.

If you do not have hills in your part of the country, improvise by running uphill on a treadmill (which also eliminates the stress of running downhill), or do your hill work on a bridge or even a multistory parking lot ramp. Hill work—whether on or off the trail—will build strength to help you run faster and tackle more difficult trails.

DISTANCE TRAINING

When you are ready to increase your trail running distance, apply the same principles as you would for increasing distance in general. Beginners might want to increase their overall mileage by 10 percent per week.

Hill repeats at 90-second intervals for a challenging workout.

An example of a training schedule for a new trail runner might be to do a long run—6 to 8 miles—on a Sunday, weight and cross train on Monday, speedwork (on the track or road) on Tuesday, weight train and cross train on Wednesday, hill repeats on Thursday, rest on Friday, and weight and cross train on Saturday. This schedule not only helps aerobic performance, but conditions for the specific challenges of running on a trail.

Once you feel comfortable running on trails and can run a solid distance at one time (6 to 8 miles), increasing distances on the trail itself is one of the most fun parts of trail running. Instead of running another mile down the road or around the block, you might explore a new trail—one that is perhaps a mile or two longer than the last—every weekend. Increasing distance, then, instead of being a purely physical challenge, can be viewed as an adventure.

BALANCE

Perhaps the biggest difference between road running and trail running is the hills. This may be the biggest difference physically, in terms of conditioning, heart rate, and endurance. But another important difference is the terrain. The beauty of trails is that they are not paved; they embrace the nature that surrounds them. This means that they are also full of challenging obstacles.

Although you might want to look around at the scenery, it is also very important to be aware of the trail under your feet. Holes, roots, rocks, and uneven ground are an

Paula Petrella

inextricable part of trail running and can cause injury: twisted ankles and knees and (if you completely wipe out) scrapes, cuts, and bruises.

Therefore, you need to keep balance in mind as you hit the trails. Your body maintains its balance by a mechanism called proprioception. Proprioceptors are tiny structures located in the joints and muscles. They deliver information from the brain to the muscles about the body's position in space, and they are part of the early warning system for impending injury. Specifically, they give the brain information about the length of a muscle and the rate at which that length is changing, the amount of resistance being generated in the muscle-tendon complex, and the position of a joint and how much stress it is bearing.

In practice, what this means is that if you are running on the trail and take a bad step on a rock, the proprioceptors in your ankle joint sense that your ankle is about to twist. They notify the brain, which in turn sends signals to the muscles on the outside of the ankle to contract and stabilize the ankle joint. The level of function of proprio-ceptors is affected by factors such as fatigue, previous injury, and aging. However, to some degree, proprioception can be learned and practiced. Along with balance-enhancing exercises such as in-line skating, Pilates, and yoga, are a few simple exercises you can practice at home.

These activities should be done for 60 seconds on each leg.

▪ With your eyes closed, balance on one leg with a slight bend in your knee.

▪ While balancing on one leg with a slight bend in your knee, randomly move the opposite leg around in the air.

TRAIL-RUNNING TECHNIQUE

The varied terrain of trail running provides great opportunities to build greater leg strength, balance, and agility. Running up-hill builds endurance and muscle strength, and running downhill quickly increases agility, balance, and proprioception. Know-ing the proper technique for running hills will keep you running efficiently and help prevent injury.

Despite the many different running styles, there is a correct way to run. Once you understand these principles and understand your current running style, you can make adjustments that allow your body to work more efficiently, thus allowing you to run farther and perhaps faster without increased effort.

Above all else, your body should be relaxed and upright. Good posture is as important in running as it is in daily life. Your arms should be relaxed at your sides, and your shoulders should not sway from side to side. Keep your head up so that your whole body is in line, with your butt tucked in. The line of your body should be perpen-dicular to the ground. Your feet should always land directly under your body. As you focus on the horizon, it should remain level and not bounce.

Many runners overstride in an attempt

Paula Petrella

Proper downhill running requires good posture.

to gain speed, which is inefficient and can lead to injuries. Speed is best gained by sharpening form, increasing leg strength, and increasing leg turnover rate. Leg turnover rate is the number of times the feet hit the ground during a specific time. On flat ground, the feet should ideally hit the ground 180 times per minute. On trails, this number may be closer to 160.

DOWNHILL RUNNING

Downhill runs are a great way to take advantage of gravity and to run faster. Continued practice on hills leads to increased confidence and enjoyment (as opposed to the fear of a wipe out!). The key to running them efficiently is to take short, fast strides. Overstriding—when the legs are too far apart—is one of the main mistakes trail runners make on downhills. Overstriding can create a breaking motion and cause strain on the knees and hips.

A very steep hill is easier to manage by slowing down and landing on a great portion of the foot, especially if you are unsure of the terrain and unaccustomed to running steep hills. If you are accustomed to running down hills and want to build up speed, run on the balls of the feet. At faster speeds this reduces pounding and allows for a quicker leg rotation, which provides greater control.

Body Position. Your upper body should be erect, with a slight forward lean. Keep your head up and tuck in your rear to make the overall bodyline perpendicular to the ground. This posture reduces the vertical force of the body landing on the ground, reducing strain on the quads. If the hill is particularly steep, run from side to side like a downhill skier, making sure to stay on the trail. Avoid running off the trail because this increases erosion and disturbs animal and plant life.

Where to Look. Keep your head erect; instead of gazing down, look a few feet ahead of you. A general "Murphy's Law" of trails is that if you are looking directly down at the root you are trying not to trip over, you'll trip over it. Look ahead and pick out the path you are going to take—your body will automatically avoid any obstacles. If there are roots and rocks that are too big to dodge, you can either jump them or slowly climb over them. Looking ahead also alerts you to curves and bends in the trail, letting you know when to adjust your speed. Shorten your stride and slow your pace to smoothly navigate switchbacks and curves.

UPHILL RUNNING

As with downhill running, body posture is essential for tackling the uphills. Keep the body perpendicular to the ground with the butt tucked in and the head erect. Focus your eyes at least 5 feet in front of you, and land with your hips directly over your feet. Short strides are the most efficient way to run uphill.

Using your Upper Body. Here's where upper-body strength training pays off. Relax, but visualize your chest and hips lifting you up the hill. Keep your chest forward, avoiding the tendency to hunch. Your arms will automatically tend to tighten up, but try to keep them relaxed. Pump your arms to the rhythm of your legs (the faster your legs move, the faster your arms should move).

Keep Breathing. You need to get enough oxygen into your lungs to compensate for the extra work your legs are doing.

Paula Petrella

Proper uphill running involves keeping good posture.

An upright chest facilitates deep breathing. If a hill becomes too steep, you can (and should) walk up the hill. Your walking posture should be the same as your running posture, with your focus on the trail ahead. Walk as long as you need to traverse the steep area—overall, walking up a steep section while taking deep breathes makes it easier for you to resume running than if you stop completely to catch your breath.

STAIRS

Trails occasionally have steps built into especially steep areas. You can either run or walk up and down the steps. The same general principles apply for navigating steps as for running trails: Keep your head up so that your whole body is perpendicular to the ground, butt tucked in, and your eyes focused several feet ahead of you. If you are afraid of falling, consider walking up and down the steps.

SNOW AND ICE

For the optimal experience, make sure your entire body (especially your feet) stays warm and dry, keep yourself adequately hydrated, and accommodate your gait for

Paula Petrella

Avoid leaning too far forward when ascending hills.

maximum traction. Keep your stride slightly shorter and avoid dark, shiny patches of ice.

CROSSING WATER

If you approach a stream and can see the bottom clearly, step quickly and lift your foot out as soon as it has touched down. A quick step can help keep your feet dry. If you are unsure how deep the water is, or if the bottom may be slippery or very uneven, cross slowly.

FALLING

A fall is an inevitable part of trail running. It is easy to get distracted by the beauty of the terrain. Trail running also includes avoiding roots, rocks, and other obstacles,

Cross streams slowly if the bottom is slippery or uneven.

so it is necessary to lift your feet high enough to clear the ground. (If you trip frequently, you may want to do leg lifts in the gym to strengthen your lifting motion.) Proper falling technique can prevent serious injuries.

To avoid falls, focus on where you are going. Look where you want to go, not where you do not want to go. Invariably, what you put into your mind is what you will get back. If you are at the end of a long run and are tired, you are more likely to fall because your concentration is low and your muscles are fatigued. On a technical or very steep trail, think positively. If you say to yourself, "Stay up, stay up," you are more likely to do so than if you repeat to yourself, "Don't fall, don't fall."

If you begin to fall, try to keep your body loose. Tensing the muscles and stiffening up makes the fall worse. The type of terrain may dictate how you choose to fall. Some runners use a tuck-and-roll method similar to that used by skydivers and martial arts practitioners. This method is useful as long as you are on ground where it is safe to roll a few feet. It may also be useful to land on the side of your body, letting your shoulder and thighs take the hit rather than your wrists, which are much more fragile. Some runners carry water bottles in their hands to break a fall and protect the wrists. You can use your arms as shock absorber if there is a safe place to put your hands.

In a fall you have little time to react. Most importantly, keep your body relaxed and try to avoid hitting sharp objects.

Practice these drills a few times a month, and falling safely will become second nature.

- One drill used in baseball training teaches you to jump to avoid obstacles. Practice on a mini-trampoline or soft grass, landing on your toes and in a slight squatting position to absorb shock. Try jumping with one foot in front of another to simulate a running position.
- Log roll: The log roll is important in learning how to fall properly. Practice by lying at the top of a hill with your chin and arms tucked into your chest, then roll down 20 to 30 feet.
- Shoulder roll: Kneel with your right knee and shin on the ground on a flat grassy area and your left foot in a slight lunge position. Then tuck your head and chin into your chest and roll onto the ground, leading with your right shoulder. You should eventually bring your feet under yourself to stand up. Then try it from a standing position.

Paula Petrella

Practice jumping over obstacles landing on your toes and in a slight squatting position.

CHAPTER 4

Recovery

Recovery is the period in your training between bouts of hard work when your muscles, joints, and other tissues are in the rebuilding phase. This recovery time is essential; you need periods when you are putting less stress on your body to allow it to rebuild so that temporary aches and pains do not become full-fledged injuries.

Remember that trail running works the muscles in different ways than road running. Running on hilly, uneven surfaces builds quadriceps, hamstrings, and calf muscles, much like doing squats and lunges in the gym. And, as when you are working out in the gym, when you run on trails, these muscle fibers break down. Rest is an important part of trail running because during the rest phase your muscles rebuild and become stronger.

◀◀ ▲ *Running near Mount Ausungate in Peru*

In training, some muscle soreness and stiffness are likely to occur. Delayed-onset muscle soreness usually occurs 48 to 72 hours after a hard workout, so you should not perform hard workouts 2 days in a row. Some runners alternate hard and easy days with 1 day per week of complete rest, and others do 1 very hard day followed by 2 easier days, without a complete rest day. Listen to your body and adjust your workouts based on how your body responds to these hard workouts. Your body will tell you which schedule is best for you.

If you feel muscle pain or soreness after a long or difficult trail run, ease off for 1 or 2 days until the soreness subsides. Stick to light cross-training or easy runs off-trail until the discomfort and soreness go away. Because trail running is a hard workout, it should make up no more than 50 percent of your total running time unless you are able to alternate with trail runs on flat ground or with short runs.

WARMING UP

In Chapter 3 we learned that the chances of injury increase when the muscles are cold, so it is important to warm up before a run. Remember that when you get up in the morning, your muscles and connective tissues are tight. By simply moving around you loosen your muscles and soft tissues and can stretch them as much as 20 percent. Ten to fifteen minutes of easy running on the trail is a sufficient warm-up before stretching.

It is important to warm up very slowly because tight muscles and tendons are easily strained. Once you have warmed up, you can focus on stretching, which,

along with cooling down after a run, is essential in keeping your body free from injury.

STRETCHING

Stretching before and after exercise is crucial. Stretching keeps all your muscles equally flexible, which can help your posture and balance and helps prevent muscle and joint injuries during trail running. Balance and posture are especially important in trail running to help stabilize your body's position on the downhills and on steep, rocky terrain. Stretching not only improves flexibility but also lessens the risk of injury by elongating the muscle fibers, relaxing the muscle, and increasing its range of motion. In the long run, this greater range of motion allows you to run with more efficiency and less expenditure of energy by using your full stride. This increased efficiency will translate into faster speeds and fewer injuries.

Runners are often confused by when to stretch: Immediately before a run? After a short warmup? Again, it is important to emphasize that before a workout, muscles can be cold and tight. Stretching a cold and shortened muscle can result in a muscle strain because the muscle's range of motion is restricted. Always warm up for 10 to 15 minutes before stretching.

Postexercise stretching is just as crucial as prerun stretching to prevent injuries. Without a stretch after a hard workout, the muscles cool down too quickly and will shorten and tighten up. This can lead to muscle cramps and stiffness. Another very important reason to stretch after exercise is to flush out lactic acid from the muscle fibers. Lactic acid is a metabolic waste product of the working muscle. The buildup of lactic acid and other waste products leads to muscle soreness later. Because stretching helps to deliver blood and oxygen to the muscles, it helps to relieve muscle soreness better than rest alone.

Paula Petrella

Figure 4.1. Calf stretch

A well-designed stretching program should target all the major muscle groups used in running and should be non–weight bearing. As you stretch, the sensation should subside gradually. If it intensifies, you are overstretching and should back off. Overstretching can cause the muscle to tighten, thus defeating your purpose.

PRE- AND POSTRUN STRETCHES

Calf stretch (Figure 4.1). Stand, leaning against a wall or tree with both hands. Put one foot in front of the other. Keep your back foot pointing straight ahead, with your heel down and your knee straight. Shift your weight forward by bending the front knee. Hold for 40 seconds, then switch legs.

Achilles stretch (Figure 4.2). In the same position as for the calf stretch, bend the extended leg slightly to stretch the Achilles area. Hold for 30 seconds, then switch legs.

Standing hamstring stretch (Figure 4.3). Stand on one leg and raise the other leg onto a bench or stump in front of you that is 18 to 36 inches high, keeping your knee straight. Rest the heel of the raised leg on the bench with your toes pointed up.

Paula Petrella

Figure 4.2. Achilles stretch

Keeping your back straight, slowly bend forward at the hip. Make sure to keep your back straight. You will feel the stretch in the raised leg. Hold for 30 seconds, then switch legs.

Groin stretch (Figure 4.4). While standing in the hamstring stretch position, turn your body 90 degrees. Bend at the hip toward the lifted leg. Hold for 30 seconds, then switch legs.

Seated variation—In a sitting position with your back erect, bend your knees and place the soles of your feet together. Place your elbows or hands on the inner knees and gently press your knees apart. Hold for 40 seconds.

Quadriceps stretch (Figure 4.5, second from left). Stand straight with your legs together, supporting yourself with one hand on a wall. Bend one knee and grasp the ankle with your free hand. Keep your thighs together and your body straight. Gently pull the ankle toward the same-side buttock. Hold for 30 seconds, then repeat with the other leg.

Recumbent variation (Figure 4.6, right)—Lie on your right side with your left leg

Figure 4.3. Standing hamstring stretch

Figure 4.4. Groin stretch

Figure 4.5. Standing quadriceps stretch (second figure from left)

bent. Grab your left ankle with your left hand and pull it toward your bottom. Hold for 30 seconds, then switch sides.

Hip flexor stretch (Figure 4.6, left). Kneel on the floor on your right knee and extend your right leg back, touching the floor with the top of your foot. Lower your hips toward the floor, making sure that your lower left leg remains perpendicular to the floor. Keep your upper body perpendicular to the ground also. Hold for 30 seconds and repeat with the other leg.

Variation—Sit with both legs straight out in front of you, then bend one leg at the knee and place the foot of the bent knee behind you. Lean back on both hands. Hold for 30 seconds and repeat for the other hip.

Hip stretch (Figure 4.7). Lie on your back and bend your knees 45 degrees. Place your feet flat on the floor, hips-width apart, then cross one leg over the other. Put your hands on the opposite knees and pull the top leg toward the opposite shoulder. Hold for 10 seconds, then release the stretch,

Figure 4.6. Hip flexor and recumbent quadriceps stretch

keeping your legs in the air. Do three times and switch legs.

Ankle rotations. Sit with your legs outstretched. Lift one leg up and bend the knee so that the hip and knee are both at 90-degree angles. Place one hand on the foot and the other on the ankle and rotate the foot 15 times each direction. Repeat with the other side.

Side stretch (Figure 4.8). Raise one arm behind your back and bend the elbow so that the hand touches the opposite shoulder. Grab the elbow with the other hand and bend at the hip in the opposite direc-

Figure 4.7. Hip stretch

tion of the raised arm. Hold for 30 seconds, then switch sides.

Scapula stretch (Figure 4.9). In a standing position, bring one arm straight across the chest with the palm turned upward. With the opposite hand, grab the elbow and pull toward the body. Hold for 30 seconds, then switch arms.

Whole body stretch. Lie on your back with arms and legs extended. Stretch your arms overhead along the floor and legs in a lengthening position, also along the floor. Hold for 5 seconds. Repeat three times.

COOLING DOWN

Just as important as warming up before exercising is cooling down when you have finished. During exercise, your muscles help pump blood from your legs to your heart and brain. When you stop, the muscle action stops, and your heart and brain suddenly get less blood and oxygen. The cooldown (any slower exercise, such as jogging or walking) helps keep blood flowing to the muscles and allows your body to work its way down from a level of high exertion to its normal resting condition. You can monitor your heart rate so that you cool down slowly until your heart has returned to its normal resting rate.

During your cooldown, take deep breaths in through your nose and out through your mouth; this will help slow down your heart rate. Your cooldown period should be at least half as long as your warmup period.

Figure 4.8. Side stretch

Figure 4.9. Scapula stretch

Cool down with a slow jog after a challenging run.

Paula Petrella

MASSAGE AND ICING

Along with warming up, stretching, and cooling down, massaging and icing your muscles are recovery techniques that keep the muscles and joints healthy between runs.

MASSAGE

The word "massage" might conjure images of a luxurious spa treatment, but simple massages are an essential part of the serious athlete's training regimen; they are not so much a luxury as a necessity in helping to rejuvenate muscles.

Massage increases blood flow to the muscle and aids in removing waste products (such as lactic acid) that contribute to muscle soreness. Rubbing a muscle that hurts is a normal response to pain and soreness.

Massage helps recuperation by restoring mobility to injured tissues. Massage and stretching can help reverse muscle spasms that can result from fatigue, strain, or postworkout soreness. Massage is also effective in working out sore areas in muscles that have been overused.

Massage is not a cure for an injury, and only a qualified health care professional can diagnose an injury. But massage therapists can help with normal postworkout pain, which is mild discomfort that disappears within a few days. If the pain lasts longer than a few days, it is an injury and should not be ignored.

Many trail runners have regular massage sessions with sports massage therapists to help detect stress and muscular imbalances even before injuries develop. The therapist then concentrates on these specific areas to relieve the stress and restore muscular balance, which helps prevent injuries.

Although massage is an important part of training, some muscle soreness can actually occur after deep massage as the natural waste products of metabolism are released from tight muscle fibers. You should allow at least 3 days after a massage before attempting any hard trail runs or events. This will give your body plenty of time to recover. It is extremely important after a deep muscle massage session to drink plenty of fluids so that the wastes released during the session can be flushed from your body.

Self-massage and partner massage are alternatives to professional massage, and you can learn some easy self-massage and partner massage techniques. The basic motions of massage use your knuckles, thumbs, and hands to create friction. Make long, smooth strokes to squeeze, lift, and compress the areas around the muscles. Make sure you can move the muscles before you start; they should be limp and relaxed. Do not work on tense or tight muscles.

In addition to using your hands, you can use a tennis ball on the buttocks or lower back by placing the ball between your back or buttocks and the wall or floor. Move up and down, pressing down on the tennis ball as it rolls over the muscle. You can even use a rolling pin on your calves and thighs.

To massage your Achilles tendons or calves, sit down with your right leg crossed over your left knee, allowing the lower leg muscles in the crossed-over right leg to relax. As you squeeze the muscles, make deep circles with your fingers or thumbs on your tendons and calves and pull with long strokes toward the center of your body or toward your heart. Repeat with the other leg.

Another self-massage technique, known as the trigger point technique, can be used for painful areas: Press the tender area

gently for 10 seconds, then release. If the pain or tightness does not subside, wait 5 minutes and then repeat for another 10 seconds, using slightly less pressure.

With this and all other self-massage techniques, once you find the origin of your pain, you can work on that area more deeply and specifically. For runners, good areas to massage are the calves, hamstrings, inner and outer thighs, buttocks, and lower back.

ICING

Many runners will sustain some type of injury during their running career. Trail runners are particularly susceptible to ankle twists, falls, and strains. With few exceptions, the initial first-aid treatment begins with RICE: rest, ice, compression, and elevation. Ice is one of the most important anti-inflammatory agents available and probably the least expensive. Heat may feel nice to a sore muscle or joint, but it will not help the healing process. Heat stimulates blood flow to the area, which increases the swelling and inflammation. Cold reaches the sore muscle or tendon and decreases the blood flow to the area, thus preventing swelling and decreasing inflammation.

For muscle soreness, you should apply ice for 15 to 20 minutes three times a day, wrapping the ice pack in a towel to protect the skin from direct contact. You should begin this as soon as you notice any muscle soreness because any time delay allows more swelling and inflammation to occur. You can either wrap ice in a towel or freeze water in a paper cup. Use the cup to

ICE PACK RECIPE

¾ cup water

¼ cup rubbing alcohol

2 resealable sandwich-size plastic bags

Put the water and alcohol into one of the resealable plastic bags, push out the bubbles, and zip it closed. Seal this bag within the second bag and freeze. Because of the alcohol, the mixture will not completely freeze but will turn into a very cold frozen slush. You can then wrap a paper towel around the slush pack before applying it to the sore area. This moist cold penetrates deeper than dry cold, so be careful that your skin does not turn white. Apply for no more than 15 minutes.

Self-made ice pack

Paula Petrella

perform ice massage: Peel off the top half of the cup and expose the ice for the massage, holding onto the wrapped bottom. You can also use a bag of frozen vegetables as an ice pack.

Commercial ice packs are readily available but tend to be either too cold or not cold enough. If they are too cold, they may burn the skin or even cause nerve damage. The commercial blue ice packs lose their coolness after 5 to 10 minutes and are not an effective treatment. For trail running, ice or ice packs should be available at the start of the run. You can carry commercial ice packs that you hit to activate on the trail for emergency use; again, these do not stay cold for very long, but they can be used in an emergency until real ice is available.

SLEEP

Your body copes with the effects of training through alternating cycles of training and rest. Although "rest" can mean light training or taking a day off from a run, total rest—sleep—is an essential part of your training program. Sleep is the time when your body recovers from the stresses placed on it during the day. Sleep is passive rest, which allows the body to repair broken-down muscles and other tissues. This repair and buildup eventually lead to an increase in overall strength and speed. A good night's sleep or a short nap after a particularly hard trail run is essential to give your body sufficient time to repair the damage sustained during the run. The American

College of Sports Medicine recommends 9 hours of sleep per night to enhance recovery, although this number varies somewhat between individuals.

If you begin your next workout without adequate rest and recovery time, your muscles and other tissues will be in a slightly weakened state. Your body can tolerate this for a short period of time, but if it goes on too long you will begin to notice signs of overtraining, such as fatigue, mood changes, alteration in sleep patterns, persistent soreness and pain, frequent cold or flu symptoms, altered appetite, poor concentration, irritability, or even injury from overuse. Extreme fatigue is not a normal part of training. It is best to get a consistent number of hours of sleep per night, although you may need additional sleep during periods of hard training.

One of the first signs of overtraining is a change in sleep patterns, particularly insomnia: the inability to sleep at night. Another indicator of overtraining is an increase in your resting heart rate. Overtraining can cause you to perform poorly in a race or even fail to finish a run. Pushing harder when the body is tired adds to fatigue and prevents complete recovery. Rather than pushing harder to improve your performance, you may need to increase your recovery time, including sleep time.

Rest is the only thing that can cure overtraining; however, you can prevent overtraining. Simply incorporate adequate sleep—including naps—and rest into your training schedule. There are several methods you can use to monitor your training so that you can intervene early with extra rest and sleep if you begin to see that you are training too hard.

A training log is an excellent method for monitoring your training and following your progress. Besides recording your daily workouts, keep a fatigue score on a scale from 0 to 5. Add the fatigue score to your training log at the end of the day, rating how you felt over the entire day, not just immediately after your workout. If you notice that your fatigue score is increasing over a few days or a few weeks and is staying higher for longer periods of time, it is probably time to add more rest to your training schedule by allowing yourself a little more sleep at night or adding a short nap into your schedule.

In addition to a fatigue scale, a pain scale is important. If you notice increasing pain and are not recovering from the pain between workouts, you are not allowing yourself enough rest time between workouts. Pain resulting from muscle soreness generally is symmetrical; you will feel the pain on both sides of your body. Pain caused by an injury, on the other hand, usually is asymmetrical. Rest is needed to resolve both muscle soreness and injury pain, but an injury also should be examined by a medical professional who can recommend necessary treatment.

Besides keeping tabs on your fatigue and pain levels, you can avoid overtraining by varying workouts according to type of exercise and length. For example, running steep trails one day and easy, flat trails the next helps minimize risk of an overuse injury. This variety allows different muscle groups to train, which gives muscles a needed change without sacrificing endurance. Design a training program that allows adequate rest, sleep, and recovery to keep you below the overtraining threshold and prevent potentially serious illness or injury.

REHYDRATION

Even experienced runners often neglect to drink enough water or other fluids during exercise, which can cause dehydration: the excessive loss of bodily fluids. Dehydration is a common result of hard exercise because the body's thirst mechanism is not an accurate gauge of its fluid needs. No matter what type of physical activity you are engaged in, it is best to drink before you feel thirsty. In addition, continue to drink after exercise for proper recovery. Drink 16 ounces of water or sports drink right after you finish running and continue to drink over the next 2 hours to replace lost body fluid.

You can estimate how much you need to rehydrate by determining your sweat rate, which can range from 1 to 4 quarts per hour. Weigh yourself before and after a timed training run. One pound of weight loss equals 1 pint, or 16 ounces of water loss. So if you lose 2 pounds in an hour, you should drink 8 ounces of water or sports drink every 15 minutes during your 1-hour runs.

Although you may not notice dehydration as much when it is cool, you still lose

Paula Petrella

Drink 5 to 10 ounces of water every 15 to 20 minutes on the trail.

plenty of water through sweating and evaporation and should continue to drink plenty of fluids. Symptoms of dehydration include headaches, side aches, muscle cramps, light-headedness or dizziness, nausea, weakness, and overall fatigue. Dehydration not only limits overall running performance but also can lead to more serious consequences including heat stroke, severe muscle cramps, disorientation, and exhaustion. Heat stroke resulting from dehydration can be fatal. If you have signs of dehydration, stop running or exercising, get to a cool place, and drink plenty of fluids.

Sports drinks containing sodium and other electrolytes can be used instead of water to replace fluid loss. There are many such sport drinks on the market, and they are designed for different uses. Some sports drinks are meant to replace electrolytes lost through sweat, such as sodium and potassium, and others are carbohydrate solutions meant to furnish energy during the run. Still others are carbohydrate replacement solutions designed to refuel exercised muscles immediately after a workout. For workouts under 1 hour, water alone is best. If you are planning to use a sports drink during a long run or race, be sure to test the drink in training first because some drinks with high carbohydrate concentrations (above 8 percent) can cause gastrointestinal upset. Some runners prefer to dilute sports drinks with 50 percent water to get the benefit of some carbohydrate and electrolyte replacement while avoiding gastrointestinal upset.

Watery foods such as salads and fruits are great for replacing fluids off the trail. They also provide valuable minerals such as potassium and magnesium. Some of the best fruits for replacement of both water and minerals are mango, papaya, cantaloupe, strawberries, oranges, tangerines, bananas, and apricots. Although the hydration value of vegetables is about the same, fresh vegetables and frozen vegetables have more nutritional value than canned vegetables, and dark and colorful vegetables are more nutritious than their pale counterparts.

Also, because salt aids in water retention, you can add salt to your food in the days preceding your long runs or races. Likewise, you can eat salted pretzels during the last half of a long trail run. Avoid using salt tablets; the sodium concentration is more than most bodies can use (and they can cause vomiting).

Nonsteroidal anti-inflammatory drugs such as aspirin, ibuprofen, and naproxen sodium should be avoided before or during a race or trail run as well because of their tendency to upset the gastrointestinal tract. If you need to use a drug for pain relief during a run, acetaminophen is safer.

NUTRITION

Diet is an integral part of any fitness program. There is much controversy and confusion regarding fad diets such as the current high-protein, low-carbohydrate "Zone" diets, and most registered dieticians and the American Heart Association do not recommend them for anyone, much less those who participate in endurance sports. According to the American Heart Association, "Some of these diets restrict healthful foods that provide essential nutrients and don't provide the variety of foods needed to adequately meet nutritional needs. People who remain on these diets very long may be at risk for inadequate vitamin and mineral intake as well as more potential health risks."

The optimal diet for both the recreational trail runner and the elite athlete is the same and centers on the three major components of food: carbohydrates, protein, and fats.

CARBOHYDRATES

Carbohydrates are essential for trail runners and other athletes because they are fuel for the muscles. Carbohydrates are the body's preferred energy source and come in two forms: simple carbohydrates, or simple sugars, and complex carbohydrates. Simple carbohydrates are found in apples, bananas, oranges, and sports drinks. Complex carbohydrates are found in pasta, oatmeal, brown rice, beans, corn, green and yellow vegetables, shredded wheat, yams, and sweet potatoes.

The 1-hour period after your workout is known as the postworkout window of opportunity because 60 to 80 percent of the replenishment of your glycogen stores takes place 1 to 3 hours after a workout. The sooner you can get carbohydrates to your muscles, the better. At this time, your body is more receptive to simple sugars, so after a run fuel up right away with the simple carbohydrates in fruits or sports drinks. At all other times, your best energy source comes from complex carbohydrates, which offer glucose to the muscles over a prolonged period of time. In addition to your carbohydrate-rich meal (or equivalent) immediately after your trail run or workout, eat a second meal 60 to 90 minutes later.

These two carbohydrate-rich meals should have 30 to 45 percent of your total calories and carbohydrates for the day. Carbohydrates should make up about 60 to 70 percent of your daily calories, and the remainder of the carbohydrates should be spaced evenly throughout the day. The ratio of carbohydrates to proteins in your meals should be about 4 grams of carbohydrates to 1 gram of protein.

PROTEIN

Protein is essential for the repair and growth of muscle tissue. Active athletes such as trail runners need more protein than sedentary people, especially in the early part of a training program. A day's protein intake should be 0.8 grams per kilogram of body weight for a healthy adult, and 1.2 to 1.7 grams per kilogram of body weight for an endurance athlete.

To calculate your weight in kilograms, divide your weight by 2.2. For example, 120 pounds divided by 2.2 equals 54.55 (55 kilograms). Protein intake should be between 10 and 20 percent of your total caloric intake for the day. Any excess protein in the body is converted to fat and does not necessarily offer additional benefits. Additionally, long-term protein consumption 20 percent over the Recommended Daily Allowance (RDA) has been linked to heart disease, some types of cancer such as colon, breast, kidney and prostate, and osteoporosis. Less protein limits the ability of your body to recover and rebuild after your workout.

As with carbohydrates, there is a window of opportunity for protein intake in the first hour after your workout. To help achieve maximum muscle growth and repair, consume 25 to 50 grams of protein immediately after a workout. The rest of your protein intake should be divided equally throughout the day. Good sources of protein are lean turkey or chicken, lean red meat, white fish, egg whites, milk, yogurt, rice, navy beans, whole grains, peanuts, peanut butter, peas, and cottage cheese. Protein can also be found in low-carbohydrate, high-protein bars and in protein powders, which can be made into shakes with low-fat milk or soy milk.

FATS

Fat is a highly concentrated form of energy. Whereas 1 gram of carbohydrate or protein provides 4 kilocalories (kcals) of energy, 1 fat gram provides 9 kcals. Your daily fat intake should make up 20 to 25 percent of your total caloric intake, and most of the fat you need should come from your natural diet.

Body fat increases when caloric intake exceeds caloric use, although studies have shown that incoming food fat is handled preferentially by the body (meaning that it ends up as body fat more readily than proteins or carbohydrates). Still, fats are an important part of the diet because of their energy content: They provide fatty acid to the cells, which the cells need to function normally. The body also needs an adequate fat intake to use certain nutrients. Fat must be present for vitamins A, D, E, and K, known as fat-soluble vitamins, to be absorbed.

Fats are not all the same, however; there are good fats, bad fats, and even worse fats. Fats generally are classified as saturated,

monounsaturated, polyunsaturated, and trans fats, which are fats that arise from monounsaturated or polyunsaturated fats and have had hydrogen atoms added to retard spoilage (called hydrogenation).

Saturated fats, the artery-clogging, bad fats, come from animal sources such as meat and dairy products and tend to raise total cholesterol and low-density lipoproteins (LDLs). Monounsaturated fats, in general, lower harmful LDLs without affecting the good, high-density lipoproteins (HDLs) and are found in olive oil and canola oil. Polyunsaturated fats, such as those found in flaxseed oil and certain fish oils, reduce the levels of both LDLs and HDLs, but they are a good source of omega-3-fatty acids, which have been shown to provide protection against blood clots. The trans fats, the worst fats, are found to a small extent in animal products but are found primarily in processed foods; they raise levels of LDLs even more than saturated fats.

Increase your intake of good fats such as olive oil, canola oil, flaxseed oil, and avocados while limiting your intake of packaged snack foods, fried foods, fast foods, and hard margarine or any other food that lists partially hydrogenated oils as a major ingredient. You should also cut back on meats and choose only low-fat dairy products.

A runner's body has higher than average caloric needs, and your diet must give your body enough energy to meet your training needs. Because fat is calorie-dense, a very low-fat diet makes it difficult to consume enough food to meet the energy demands of your body. If your calculated fat intake is below 20 percent, or if you think your fat intake may be extremely low, you can take 1 tablespoon of flaxseed, olive, or safflower oil or eat a handful of peanuts once a day to make sure you are getting some of the essential fatty acids that play an important role in growth, recovery, and day-to-day well-being.

FIBER

Fiber is the structural part of plants and is found in vegetables, fruits, grains, and legumes. Both soluble and insoluble fiber provide important health benefits. Adequate fiber intake lowers blood cholesterol, keeps the large intestine healthy, helps prevent colon cancer, diabetes, appendicitis, and diverticulosis. Wheat bran, for example, reduces the bile acids that are known to promote cancer in the colon. You should eat 20 to 35 grams of fiber per day. The average intake in the U.S. is about half that.

Breakfast is one of the most important meals of the day and is also a good opportunity to incorporate high-fiber foods such as bran cereal, oatmeal, whole bran muffins,

---

SEVEN GUIDELINES FOR A HEALTHY DIET

- Eat a variety of foods to get the energy, protein, vitamins, minerals, and fiber you need for good health.
- Balance the food you eat with physical activity to maintain or improve your weight and reduce your chances of developing high blood pressure, heart disease, stroke, certain cancers, and diabetes.
- Choose a diet with plenty of grain products, vegetables, and fruits, which provide needed vitamins, minerals, fiber, and complex carbohydrates and can help lower your fat intake.
- Choose a diet low in fat, saturated fat, and cholesterol to reduce your risk of heart attack and certain types of cancer and to help you maintain a healthy weight.
- Choose a diet moderate in sugars. A diet with a lot of sugar has too many calories and too few nutrients for most people.
- Choose a diet moderate in salt and sodium to help reduce your risk of high blood pressure.
- Drink alcoholic beverages in moderation. Alcohol supplies calories but no nutrients.

—Developed by the U.S. Department of Agriculture and the Department of Health and Human Services

and whole wheat waffles into your diet. Putting fruit on your cereal will add a little more fiber.

Eating a variety of foods helps you consume a mix of both soluble and insoluble fibers, which are both beneficial. Because whole grains are full of fiber, consider switching to whole grain breads, cereals, buns, bagels, and pasta. Breads with whole grain include cornbread from whole ground cornmeal, cracked wheat bread, oatmeal bread, pumpernickel bread, rye bread, and whole wheat bread. High-fiber snacks include popcorn, fresh fruit, raw vegetables, and nuts. Fruits and vegetables provide water as well as fiber. Eat at least five servings of fruits and vegetables per day, including the skin, if possible. Most of the fiber is found in the skin and pulp, so choose the whole fruit instead of the juice. You can also substitute higher-fiber ingredients in recipes by using whole wheat flour in baked foods. Look for foods with "high in fiber" or "fiber rich" on the label.

Generally, it is not when you eat but how much you eat that determines your weight. Your body needs a certain number of calories for its daily activities, regardless of when you eat them. Neverless, eating smaller, more frequent meals throughout the day and evening actually promotes overall growth and muscle rebuilding. Because weight gain results from consuming more calories than your total energy needs, the best way to maintain both health and fitness is to eat well-planned, regular meals and nutritious snacks throughout the day and into the evening.

UNDERSTANDING METABOLIC RATE AND NUTRITIONAL NEEDS

Balancing the carbohydrates, fats, and proteins helps your body produce the energy needed to maintain the lifestyle of a healthy athlete. But you also have to know how *much* food to eat to stay energetic and active. You burn calories during activity and at rest. The energy needed to maintain the body at rest is known as basal metabolism. Basal metabolic rates differ among people and is affected by factors such as the ratio of muscle to fat in your body, exercise activity, age, height, stress, environmental factors such as temperature, and more. A person with a low basal metabolic rate may gain weight more easily and have a harder time losing weight than someone whose metabolic rate is relatively high.

The higher the ratio of muscle tissue to fat, the faster the metabolic rate. Someone with more muscle uses more energy per minute and is less likely to store food energy as fat than a person with a lower metabolic rate. Even at rest, the person with a higher metabolism is burning more calories.

It is possible to increase metabolism by doing aerobic exercise regularly, which also helps speed the digestive process so that fewer calories are absorbed. Resistance exercises also help replace flab with muscle—a beneficial change because your body must use more of its energy (burn more calories) to maintain muscle than fat. Muscle weighs more than fat, but it raises your metabolism, helping to tone and define your body and improving your strength. As we age, our basal metabolic rate becomes progressively slower. Consequently, we need about two percent fewer calories each passing decade to maintain the same body weight.

Your everyday eating habits affect metabolic levels as well. Strenuous diets should be avoided. The lower your daily caloric intake, the more slowly your metabolism runs because your body perceives it as a starvation threat. If you want to lose weight, you can decrease your daily calorie count by 500 calories (at most!) to safely lose one pound per week

CALCULATING YOUR IDEAL DAILY DIET

To accurately determine your daily energy needs, you will need to factor in your Basal Metabolic Rate (BMR) and daily activity level. BMR can be estimated by using the following quick formula:

Men: Weight in kg x 24 = calories needed per day
Women: Weight in kg x 23 = calories needed per day
(To determine weight in kilograms, divide weight in pounds by 2.2)

A slightly more accurate (but complicated formula) to determine BMR:

Men: 66 + (13.7 x weight in kg) + (5 x height in cm) – (6.8 x age in years) = BMR
Women: 655 + (9.6 x weight in kg) + (1.8 x height in cm) – (4.7 x age in years) = BMR
(To determine height in centimeters, multiply height in inches x 2.54)

Now multiply that number by 2.1 for men or 1.9 for women and this number will give you the needed calories per day to maintain weight and energy needs for moderate activity levels.

To determine the amount of protein, carbohydrates, and fat in your daily diet:
Protein: daily calories x 15 to 20 percent = total protein calories per day; divide this number by four to get the grams of protein per day.
Carbohydrates: daily calories x 60 to 70 percent = total carbohydrate calories per day; divide this number by four to get the grams of carbohydrates per day.
Fats: daily calories x 20 to 25 percent = total fat calories per day; divide this number by nine to get the grams of fat per day.

for greater long-term success. Another way to help raise your metabolism is to eat breakfast. Research has shown that people who skip breakfast have lower metabolic rates than those who eat breakfast regularly. Moderate eating throughout the day revs your system. Reducing fat and increasing carbohydrate intake will help stimulate the metabolism because complex carbohydrates are the body's preferred energy source. Although they contain more calories per gram, fats are not as useful as an energy source. Low-fat foods such as whole grain breads and cereals, vegetables, fruits, potatoes, and pasta are best for your metabolism.

WHAT TO EAT BEFORE A RUN

For any trail run lasting more than 2 hours, it is good to eat something simple such as toast or a bagel a couple of hours before. Also, be sure to eat well the night before and immediately after the run.

What you eat before you work out should give you fuel and energy, and should not impede your effort. Give yourself enough time for the food to digest after you eat, generally 1 hour for a snack and 3 to 6 hours for a full meal. If you are going to run hard, allow even more time for digestion.

For your prerun meals, choose easily digestible foods, which have high starch content and low fat content, such as breads and pastas. Avoid juice unless it is consumed at least 2 hours before a workout. It contains fructose, a sugar known to cause stomach upset.

CAFFEINE

Caffeine is a common additive in products such as sports gels and bars. Despite extensive research on the use of caffeine and athletic performance, the exact role of caffeine as a performance-enhancing drug is still controversial. There is general agreement that caffeine does not benefit short-term, high-intensity exercise such as sprinting, but it seems to enhance performance in endurance sports. One of the reasons for this is that caffeine mobilizes fat stores and encourages working muscles to use the fat as a fuel. This delays the depletion of glycogen and allows the exercise to continue for a longer period of time. The critical time period for glycogen use seems to be during the first 15 minutes of exercise, and caffeine has been shown in several studies to decrease this initial glycogen use by as much as 50 percent.

Of course, there is also a downside to the use of caffeine, and you should consider the potential side effects before you decide to use it as a performance enhancer. Differences in metabolism, diet, and frequency of caffeine use are some factors that can determine how you will react to it. As with anything that is new, you need to try it first in small quantities to see how your body reacts. Some athletes may actually have a decrease in performance, which is usually caused by the side effects of the caffeine.

Caffeine is a mild diuretic and increases fluid loss from the body. Even though caffeine does not appear to significantly alter water balance or body temperature during exercise, dehydration is a potential concern,

RECOMMENDATIONS REGARDING CAFFEINE BENEFITS

- Ingest caffeine about 3 to 4 hours before the trail run. Although the levels of caffeine in your blood will peak much sooner, the maximum caffeine effect on fat stores appears to occur several hours after the peak blood levels.

- Consider decreasing or abstaining from caffeine for 3 to 4 days before the trail run. This reduces caffeine tolerance and maximizes the effect of the caffeine. However, be aware of potential caffeine withdrawal symptoms such as headaches and tremors.

- Make sure you have used caffeine in a variety of prior training and running conditions to determine how your body will react to its use. Never try anything new on the day of an important trail run.

- Remember that caffeine is a drug; you must decide whether it is something you want to use. If you take prescription medication, check with your doctor about the use of caffeine and its potential effects on your overall health before using it.

especially in ultraendurance events. Caffeine can also cause large intestine contractions, leading to cramping and diarrhea, which can also lead to dehydration.

The International Olympic Committee lists caffeine as a restricted drug. However, urinary levels up to a concentration of 12 milligrams per liter are acceptable (you would need about eight cups of coffee to exceed this level). Also consider that the rate of caffeine clearance from the body can vary, and different people metabolize it at different rates.

CHAPTER 5

Jon Collard

Environmental Factors, Navigation, and Safety

Trail running is a great adventure, and care and planning are necessary to ensure that you have a safe and comfortable run, whether on a vacation or in your neighborhood. You are ultimately responsible for your own safety. In this chapter we discuss important safety issues such as permits and reservations, trail etiquette, communication, navigation, weather, and plants and animals.

When traveling to a trailhead, leave valuables at home, park in designated areas, and keep the car locked. Obey all posted regulations, whether on public or private lands. If you plan to run on private land, get permission from the owner first. Many trails traverse both public and private lands. Just as you would not want someone in your house unannounced, so should you respect other's property. If you come across

◀◀ ▲ *Advance planning allows a carefree trail run.*

wildlife or livestock, stay a safe distance away and do not disturb them. You may want to limit your running to areas where hunting is prohibited.

Stay on marked and existing trails. If you approach a fork in the trail, use the most worn trail. Most trail routes are designed to drain water and minimize soil erosion and vegetation loss. Often state and national parks managers reroute trails to preserve the integrity of the environment and protect an area from becoming too heavily traveled. Stay off all closed trails because they may be closed for safety and land protection reasons.

PERMITS AND RESERVATIONS

If you are traveling to a trail site, check in advance regarding any required permits.

You will first need to determine whether the land is managed by the U.S. Forest Service (USFS), the National Park Service (NPS), the Bureau of Land Management (BLM), or a state park. Some private lands, such as those managed by conservancies, also require usage permits. Many popular trailheads limit the number of people allowed to enter the wilderness areas. These quotas may be year-round, or they may be in effect during a specific season. Some permits are issued strictly by advance reservation, and some are issued on a first-come, first-served basis. In extremely popular areas, such as the Mount Whitney Trail in California, applications generally are accepted during a one-month period for the entire season and are issued by a lottery system. If you are in a permit-required area, keep your permit handy. Often, rangers will ask to see them. If you are in a group, each member should keep a copy.

Some of the revenues for these fees pay for trail maintenance and improvements, trash removal, and, in some cases, the cost of search and rescues.

TRAIL ETIQUETTE

Trails are enjoyed by many types of people and for many different uses. Always be gracious to others and respect their desire to enjoy trails. To accommodate increased usage on trails by mountain bikers, equestrians, and hikers, some rules have been established to minimize conflict and preserve the integrity of trails. Be considerate and respectful in all situations.

On multiaccess trails, pedestrians should yield to equestrians, and cyclists should yield to all other trail users. As a general rule, the uphill traveler should yield to one going downhill. Momentum dictates that it is easier for the person going uphill to stop. However, there are times when it may make more sense to yield to a biker who is struggling up a hill. If there is any doubt about your safety or the safety of others, always yield as a courtesy. If you are passing another person from behind, alert them in advance with your voice. Do not use bells or whistles.

When running with a group on a narrow trail, run single file and leave enough room for others to pass. You should stay to the right and pass on the left when others are on the trails. Pass only when you can clearly see the trail in front of you. If you encounter cyclists or equestrians, be considerate and let them know how many people are behind you (see Appendix A, Responsible Trail Running Guidelines).

If you encounter horses on the trail, stand quietly as they pass and do not make sudden movements; some animals are easily spooked. Talk in calm, quiet tones. A red ribbon on a horse's tail indicates that it may kick if approached too closely from behind.

Paula Petrella

Stay to one side of the trail when running in a group.

If you are in a residential area headed for a trail early in the morning, remember to keep the noise level down as neighbors may be sleeping. We strongly discourage the use of headphones on the trail because they limit your ability to hear others approaching on the trail and compromise your safety. Also, they prevent you from enjoying sounds of the trail, such as birds chirping. If you see trail damage, such as washed-out areas or downed trees, report it to the park's maintenance system or a ranger.

ENVIRONMENTAL AWARENESS

One of the greatest problems on trails is erosion. Erosion results from human activity as well as natural forces, such as wind and precipitation. Fires can also contribute. When soil erodes, it ends up in streams and rivers, where it can pollute water and disrupt spawning areas. Additionally, the removal of valuable topsoil reduces plant life, which accelerates erosion further. It can take hundreds of years for land to

Obey all posted signs.

Paula Petrella

reform naturally. In fact, in tropical and temperate areas, it takes an average of 500 years to renew 1 inch of topsoil.

Areas most susceptible to erosion are those that have steep slopes, have been subject to recent fires, have very muddy or dusty trails, or have had heavy or consistent rains. Avoid these areas. If you come across mud puddles, snow patches, or wet spots, carefully run through them, not around them. Also, jump or step over any fallen trees. Running around them can cause trails to widen, increasing soil and vegetation damage.

In arid regions, avoid stepping on cryptobiotic soil, which is a living organism made up of lichens, moss, and algae. Cryptobiotic soil helps build valuable fertile soil, prevents erosion, and retains moisture. You can recognize it by its lumpy appearance, and it may be black, green, or white. If stepped on, it can easily blow away in the wind and take five to fifty years to grow back.

LITTERING AND BATHROOM ETIQUETTE

Always leave a natural environment as you found it, and minimize your impact. Take only photographs and enjoyable memories of your run. Leave only footprints. Never litter. Pack it in, pack it out, which means that any materials you bring in should leave with you. Even if there are nearby trash cans, reducing waste management costs leaves more funds for other purposes, such as trail preservation.

Use established backcountry toilets when available. Bury feces at least 200 feet from any water source and at least 6 inches deep in the soil. To do so, dig a hole with a branch or stick and cover with dirt and leaves or whatever brush is nearby. Dispose of liquid waste at least 200 feet away from a water source because it can contaminate water and affect nearby wildlife. Always pack out your toilet paper, sanitary napkins, and tampons. Resealable plastic bags work well for this.

COMMUNICATION

Whether your trail run is a few hundred feet from your door or hundreds of miles away, let someone at home know where you are going and when you will be back, and leave a map or description of your anticipated route. If you are driving to a trailhead, leave a note on your car indicating when you expect to return. If there is a log book at the ranger station, be sure to sign in upon arrival and out upon departure.

Communication between runners on the trail is also important. Many running groups use two-way radios between the first and last runner to keep track of the group. Two-way radios work at distances up to 4 miles; however, they are less effective in mountainous or hilly terrain. If you use electronic devices, remember to take an extra set of batteries. On group trail runs, stop and wait for slower runners at predetermined junctions such as stream crossings, bridges, or trail intersections.

It is always a good idea to run with others, but if you are running alone, carry a cell phone. Turn it off to save the battery; it can be a lifesaver if you become injured or lost.

NAVIGATION

Although many of the trails you choose might be in familiar places and easily navigable, at some point you may be in an area where you need navigational skills.

Even on familiar trails, there may be an unexpected fork in the trail that is not indicated on a map. As mentioned earlier, managed trails often are rerouted to preserve the environment.

To avoid getting lost, you need to know where you are, in what direction you are facing, and where you want to go. There are many tools to help you navigate, including maps, compasses, altimeters, and global positioning systems (GPS) as well as resources found in nature.

Paula Petrella

Navigating using GPS, map, and compass

MAP READING

One of the most effective ways to navigate is with a map. Up-to-date topography (topo) maps are excellent guides for planning runs and navigating on the trail. They are the best way to predict the terrain, indicating whether the trail is a fire road or single track, whether it has hills and water crossings, and the distance. USFS maps and tourist maps can provide valuable additional details and, if available, should be used in conjunction with topo maps. Check the publication date and make sure it is current. Trails and terrain can change drastically even from year to year, especially after periods of heavy precipitation. If you are traveling in an unfamiliar area, check with the management agency for any changes.

Maps contain keys that indicate types of trails (such as maintained, nonmaintained, and fire roads) and may specify whether bikes or horses are allowed. You can get a good idea of the terrain by learning to recognize how certain land features are represented on maps. Topo maps indicate the distance between contour lines; 50 or 100 feet is a common interval distance. However, any cliffs or ridges between contour lines may not be indicated. For example, if your map has 50-foot contour lines and there is a 40-foot dropoff that falls between the lines, be aware that it will not be indicated.

Also note that the closer together the contour lines, the steeper the hill. Contour lines indicate whether a hill is convex (steeper at the bottom and flattens out at

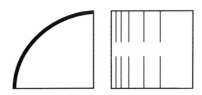

Figure 5.1. Convex Slope. You cannot see the top of a convex slope from the bottom, and climbers may be frustrated by meeting a succession of false summits. The contour lines representing a convex slope are close together at the foot of the slope and spread out toward the top.

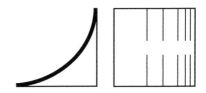

Figure 5.2. Concave Slope. You can see the summit of a concave slope from the bottom, and at the bottom it has a gentle gradient. On a map, the contour lines of the slope bunch up together toward the top, so you can expect the climb to grow steeper as you approach the summit.

Figure 5.3. Valley. On a map, the contours of a river valley appear as a series of V shapes.

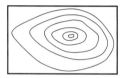

Figure 5.4. Hill. A hill is recognizable as a series of concentric rings.

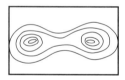

Figure 5.5. Saddle. A saddle, which is a depression between two hills, appears as two sets of circles joined by curving contour lines.

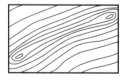

Figure 5.6. Ridge. Ridges appear as fingers of close, parallel contours, often with closed contours indicating high peaks.

top) or concave (flatter at the bottom and steeper as it rises).

See Figures 5.1 through 5.6 for land features and landmarks commonly shown on topographic maps.

Before you start your run, identify where you are on the map. Plot out your course on the map and try to visualize the terrain you will be running; some common map symbols are shown in Figure 5.7. (One of the best ways to improve your map-reading skills is to bring a map to an area you are already familiar with.) Follow the course on the map before the run and visualize what it looks like.

Once on the trail, stop periodically and check your location on the map. Keep the map handy so you can refer to it often. Keep it protected in a plastic sleeve, or use a laminated map for protection from moisture. Make mental notes of landmarks such as peaks, valleys, and rivers as you pass. With continued practice, your map-reading skills may prevent you from getting lost, and you will be better equipped to plan future trail runs.

If you are already on the trail and are unsure of your location, climb to a nearby hill or peak to find a point of reference such as a valley, river, or saddle. Position the north side of the map facing north and rotate your body until it matches what you see in front of you.

USING A COMPASS

If you are certain that conditions will remain clear, and if you plan on staying only on marked trails or fire roads, a map

POINT SYMBOL EXAMPLES:

■ Building

✖ Mine

○~ Spring

●—● Gate

⊟ Bridge

▲ Campground

🛆 Picnic area

🛖 Ranger station

LINE SYMBOL EXAMPLES:

〜〜 Watercourse - year round (in blue)

- - ⁄ - - Watercourse - intermittent (in blue)

═══ Improved road

+—+—+—+ Railroad

⎵ \ - - - - ⌐ Trail

—・—・—・- Boundary

SURFACE SYMBOL EXAMPLES:

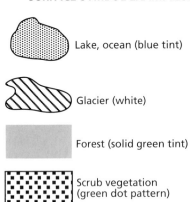

Lake, ocean (blue tint)

Glacier (white)

Forest (solid green tint)

Scrub vegetation (green dot pattern)

Figure 5.7. Map key

often is all you need for navigation. If visibility is reduced by cloud cover, rain, snow, or dense vegetation, you will find a compass to be an invaluable tool. Carry a compass with you on any course with which you are not familiar. A bright, sunny morning can quickly become cloudy if you climb into the clouds and find yourself disoriented after a few switchbacks and no longer know which direction is north.

There are two compass types: protractor and prismatic. Either type is adequate for basic orienteering. Additionally, some altimeter watches feature an electronic compass readout. On hand-held compasses, the red needle always points to Earth's magnetic north pole. On most compasses, the housing has a scale that ranges from 0 to 360. Those are the degrees, or bearings. Before navigating, you need to know the area's magnetic declination, which is the difference between magnetic north (the direction toward Earth's magnetic north pole) and true north (the direction toward Earth's geographic north pole). Magnetic declination varies according to position and can be affected by iron in the ground, a nearby vehicle, or metal objects you are carrying. In North America, the magnetic declination ranges from about 20 degrees east to 20 degrees west. In the west, magnetic declination is to the east. Maps indicate both true north and the magnetic declination.

To more accurately determine your location using a compass, place the compass on the map and turn the map until the north–south grid lines are parallel to the compass needle. Turn the map again until the needle of the compass indicates magnetic declination.

For example, suppose you have determined where north is, and you want to go northwest because you know there is a large landmark, such as a fire road, river, or main trail. Turn the compass housing so northwest is exactly where the direction of the travel arrow meets the housing. Be sure to hold the compass flat for accuracy; it is very important that the red needle continues to point north. Then head in the direction of the travel arrow. You should check your bearing at least every 100 meters. This technique is most useful for determining general direction.

USING AN ALTIMETER

Many watches contain an altimeter, which is a useful tool in navigation. These altimeters measure elevation by recording barometric pressure and then calculating altitude. As you gain elevation, atmospheric pressure decreases; as you lose elevation, pressure increases. As you run, the difference in pressure is detected by the altimeter and

Paula Petrella

A watch which features a compass and an altimeter

converted to elevation, which can assist you when you are locating your position on a map.

Because the altimeter data are based on barometric pressure, weather affects your reading. Most altimeters can drop even when there is no change in elevation. You may find after an overnight camp that your altimeter indicates you have dropped 100 to 200 feet. In unstable weather, the reading can drop as much as 500 feet. You can compensate for the weather changes in pressure by calibrating the elevation in your altimeter at known elevations. For example, set your altimeter at the start of a run and at other known elevations, which you can obtain from a topo map. If you are staying overnight, you may want to record the altimeter reading at night, then reset it in the morning. Complete instructions on using an altimeter are included with the unit, and you should study them before attempting to use the altimeter.

USING GPS

The maritime industry has used global positioning systems (GPS) for years, and using them has recently become very popular with hikers and trail runners. The GPS unit uses a worldwide network of radio signals, which are reflected back to Earth by satellites to help determine your position, with accuracy to within 50 feet.

A GPS receiver will give you your location in terms of latitude and longitude or Universal Transverse Mercator (UTM) coordinates, which are indicated on most maps printed within the last ten years. You can program the coordinates of your destination into the GPS, and the receiver will indicate the distance and compass bearing.

Use of GPS receivers may be limited in deep canyons, on hillsides, or under heavy forest cover. Additionally, GPSs are battery operated and may not work correctly in temperatures at or below freezing. For these reasons, GPS should be used as an additional tool in navigation, not in place of a map and compass.

NAVIGATING BY NATURE

If you find yourself lost and without a map, compass, or GPS, you can still determine direction. The information in this section refers to the Northern Hemisphere. The sun is one of the easiest ways to calculate directions. In the summer, it rises in the northeast and sets in the northwest. In winter, it rises in the southeast and sets in the southwest. On the equinoxes in March and September, the sun rises and sets due east and west, and at noon, the shadows fall to the north.

Typically the north face of a tree is more humid than the south face, so lichen or moss is more likely to appear on the north side. During winter, snow melts faster on south-facing slopes. Vegetation and plants usually are thicker on south-facing slopes, and ants are also more likely to build nests on the south side of a tree. In nature, an evergreen tree that is not surrounded by other trees will be bushier on the south side. Birch and poplar trees have the lightest bark on the south side and the darkest on the north.

You can also use your watch if it has hour and minute hands instead of a digital read-out. Turn the watch so the hour hand points in the direction of the sun (Figure 5.8). Draw an imaginary line between the hour hand and the 12 o'clock position on the dial. South is halfway between that line and the 12 o'clock position on your watch. During daylight savings time, the north–south line is found halfway between the hour hand and the 1 o'clock position on the dial.

If you find yourself on the trail at night, find the North Star (Figure 5.9). If you draw an imaginary line from the two stars in front of the front of the Big Dipper (A) and continue about four or five times the distance (B), you will find the North Star. It is within 2 degrees of true north.

If you run in the late afternoon, you may want to determine how much sunlight is left. Should you do that extra 5-mile loop? To calculate when the sun will hit the horizon, hold your hand away from you at arm's length and put your fingers parallel to the horizon. Count the number of fingers that fit between the horizon level and the sun. Each finger represents about 10 to 12 minutes.

Continued practice with a variety of navigational tools is the best way to ensure good skills, and the more tools you can use successfully, the safer you will be.

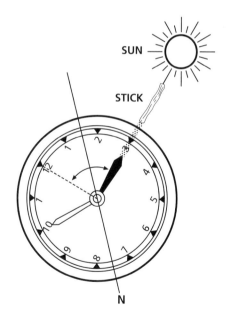

Figure 5.8. Calculating direction using a watch

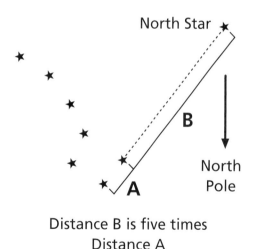

Distance B is five times Distance A

Figure 5.9. Determining direction using the North Star

GETTING LOST
(OR GETTING FOUND)

On the trail, it is easy to be distracted by the magic of the environment. Enjoy your surroundings, but also be mindful of where you are. Pay attention to trail junctions and landmarks. Trail intersections may be marked clearly with a post describing mileage and trail name, or they may be indicated only by a hidden, less worn path covered by vegetation. Avoid getting on the wrong trail, wondering where you are an hour later.

If the trail is covered by snow or overgrown with vegetation, it may be difficult to see. Look for marks on the trees such as slashes in the trunk or trees painted with yellow or orange spots or tied with ribbons. You can also look for signs of pruning where maintenance has cleared the trail for better accessibility. To avoid getting lost and to minimize your impact on the environment, stay on the trail.

WEATHER

Before any trail run, you should check for possible weather condition changes. Weather is particularly changeable in the mountains and near large bodies of water. Depending on the area and the time of year, weather can change suddenly. Check with the National Oceanic and Atmospheric Administration, which is a parent of the National Weather Service. It broadcasts weather conditions continuously on 380 stations in the United States using frequencies from 162.40 MHz to 162.55 MHz FM.

Local topography can also affect weather. Higher levels of precipitation occur on mountains and on high windward slopes. Temperatures typically cool as elevation increases (3.5 degrees Fahrenheit for every 1,000 feet of elevation in dry, stable air and up to 5.5 degrees Fahrenheit in moist, unstable air).

While on the trail, you can do your own forecasting by recognizing cloud patterns. Cloud formations are determined by temperature, pressure, and moisture content. You should look in the direction of the prevailing winds to anticipate the weather. Also, a sudden drop in temperature and change in wind can mean that a storm is approaching. A storm is likely to occur if you see nimbostratus clouds, which are dark gray and have a ragged base. If cloud formations move lower and lower and change from high, wispy clouds (cirrus) to thicker, gray clouds (altostratus) to low, shallow, gray clouds (stratus), then precipitation is likely. A quickly lowering barometric pressure also indicates a change in weather.

The following types of cloud formations are categorized by their altitude and shape:
- Cirrus (high)—High, wispy clouds; usually indicate fair weather
- Nimbus (rain cloud)—Large, towering, dark; can indicate rain or hail
- Cumulus (heap)—Drifting, puffy, and white; fair as long as form stays
- Stratus (flat, layered)—Low, shallow, gray; can indicate light mist or drizzle

DESERT RUNS

Running through the desert can be a magical experience. What seems from afar to be a harsh, colorless, and lifeless stretch of land becomes a fascinating tour of bizarre vegetation and land and rock formations. Spend time in the desert, and you realize how full of life it is—from brilliantly colored cactus flowers to lizards, birds, bats, and coyotes. Up close, rock formations reveal shades of pink, orange, and brown. A short climb in elevation affords vast views of endless skies and wide-open spaces.

The desert is a delicate environment, and you must take care to protect your own safety and the fragile ecosystem. The two most crucial concerns in desert running are staying hydrated and keeping the body cool, especially during warmer weather.

Before a desert run, calculate your water needs and determine what sources are available. Water sources such as rivers or lakes indicated on maps may be seasonal or nonexistent. Natural water sources are hard to come by. In addition, water may be too alkaline or salty to drink, or it may be contaminated. Be sure to carry enough water for the time you will be running (see Chapter 2), or arrange to obtain water on the run by caching the water in advance or running by a known water source. In warmer temperatures, you may drink up to 2 gallons per day. You should also keep extra water in your car for after the run.

To stay cool in the desert and other hot climates, wear the proper clothing (as described in Chapter 2), taking care to protect the skin from exposure to the sun. You can also prepare your body to run in warmer temperatures by gradual acclimation.

According to *Running Research News,* you can become fully acclimated after 7 days of hot weather training, but only to the extent of the conditions in which you have trained. Research suggests that as long as your training is fairly intense (e.g., 85 percent of maximum heart rate or above), running just 30 minutes per day for about one week will acclimate you to running in hot weather. You can also simulate heat by overdressing and running at midday, but take care to avoid overheating or dehydration.

On desert runs, shade may be hard to come by. If you need a break from the sun, look for a cave or use an emergency blanket to create shade. Be aware that flash flooding can occur in canyons and washes. Flooding is worst in dry areas where the surface of the ground is hard packed. Stay out of canyons where there is no quick escape route unless you are certain there is no possibility of flash flooding. Runoff can travel from a rain source miles away. Only fit and experienced trail runners should attempt warm weather desert running.

Racers try to keep cool in the desert heat.

A rainbow in the morning indicates showers to come. Seen late in the day, it indicates clear weather. A red or orange sky in the morning indicates rain or snow. In the evening, it indicates the approach of good weather.

LIGHTNING AND THUNDERSTORMS

Lightning occurs when rising warm air meets cold air, and static electricity is created as water in the clouds becomes agitated. The thunder you hear after a strike is the acoustic shock wave created by the electrical discharge. Even if the sky above you is sunny, lightning can strike from a storm up to 15 miles away. Lightning is more likely to occur closer to the equator and in mountainous areas. It is also most likely to occur in North America between June and September.

If lightning strikes within 6 to 8 miles, take immediate cover. To gauge how far away a storm is, count the number of seconds between the sound of the thunder and the flash. For every 5 seconds, the lightning is 1 mile away. According to the National Lightning Safety Institute:

- Seek clumps of shrubs or trees of uniform height.
- Seek ditches, trenches, or low ground.
- Assume a low, crouching position with feet together.
- Avoid water, metallic objects, and high ground.
- Avoid tall, solitary trees.
- If with others, spread out 15 to 20 feet apart.
- Avoid open spaces.

Ken Dewey, research climatologist at the University of Nebraska, adds that you should walk because running can create static electricity that attracts lightning. Although lightning strikes cannot be predicted, taking these steps will reduce the likelihood of getting struck on the trail.

ANIMALS

Most of us see nondomesticated animals only on a trip to the zoo or while hiking or camping in remote wilderness. Trail running gives us the opportunity to enjoy animal encounters, which are another reminder of the life and energy that exist in the great outdoors and are both a delight and a source of danger. Remember to appreciate and respect the animals' habitat. You are a visitor in their home, where they hunt for food, raise their young, sleep, and play.

As we develop more and more land that was once animal habitat, animals are forced to live in smaller areas, so contact becomes more likely. Some deer in the United States live their whole lives in a five-block area of a residential neighborhood. Grizzly bears, which used to occupy areas from the Midwest to California, now occupy only about 2 percent of their original range.

In the United States, the large animals you are most likely to encounter are bears, mountain lions, cougars, bison, elk, moose, mountain goats, or deer. Smaller animals, such as raccoons, bobcats, opossums, wolves, coyotes, skunks, porcupines, foxes, and snakes are also common. As a rule, animals are most active at sunrise and dusk and at night. You are also more likely to meet them when the trails are less busy, such as during the week.

A little common sense goes a long way. You should never feed or approach animals. Most animals will not attack unless they feel threatened, although wild animals of all kinds are unpredictable. Animals that look tame or approachable can become instantly aggressive, especially if they feel threatened or have babies nearby. Wildlife experts recommend staying at least 100 yards away from bears and at least 25 yards away from smaller animals. Animals are like people in that they have different moods and can behave differently on any given day.

Getting too close to animals may also endanger them. They can lose footing and fall, get separated from their young, abandon dens or nests, become vulnerable to other predatory animals, or abandon an important food source.

BEARS

Perhaps no other animal incites as much fear as bears. In the United States, grizzly bears and black bears inhabit many parts of the West. Grizzly bears grow to about 7 feet tall and weigh 400 to 600 pounds, but larger males can grow up to 800 pounds. Their smaller and usually less aggressive counterparts are the black bears. Black bears weigh 100 to 300 pounds, grow to about 5 feet tall when standing on hind legs, and may be black, brown, cinnamon, or blond. Both species live in forests and mountain areas and usually head toward lower elevations in the spring. They live under fallen or hollowed-out trees and in caves. Like most other animals, bears generally avoid human contact, but they may charge if they feel threatened or if there are cubs nearby. Especially when in bear country, do not travel alone. Bears often travel on the same paths you might: on animal trails, along ridges, and along water. Be aware of wind direction. Bears have an excellent sense of smell, and if the wind is at your back, a nearby bear probably will smell you and leave the area. If the wind is in your face, an encounter is more likely. If you come across an animal carcass, you should leave the area immediately. Bears often feed for days on them.

Although all wild animals are unpredictable, you should understand the body language of bears to help you determine what to do if you encounter one. If a bear turns away from you or swings his head from side to side, he is looking for a way out of the situation. Bears usually stand on all fours, but a bear may stand on its hind legs to survey what is nearby or sniff the air. This in itself is not an aggressive posture. Signs of aggression can be any or all of the following: direct eye contact, ears pulled back, paws at the ground, or a woofing or huffing noise. If you encounter a bear and he is not charging, remember the following:

- Stay calm. Do not run. To do so can trigger a chase response. Bears can run 30 to 35 miles per hour, faster than Olympic sprinters. Back away slowly. Do not turn your back to a bear.
- Look passive and avert your eyes. Direct eye contact is a sign of aggression. You want to show that you are not a threat.
- Speak in a calm, monotone voice. Make human noise.
- Do not make wild or frantic movements.
- If a bear charges you, it is probably a bluff charge meaning it may come

Stay at least 100 yards away from bears.

Clickart ©Broderbund

straight for you, then veer away at the last moment. Bears usually charge if they consider you a threat. Bears that have no experience with humans may charge because they see you as prey. If you are charged:

- Roll into a ball or lie flat on the ground and protect your face and neck.
- Be still. The bear usually stops attacking when it believes you are no longer a threat.
- If it continues to attack, you may need to fight back. Use any possible weapons, such as rocks or sticks, and aim for the bear's eyes, nose, and mouth.

MOUNTAIN LION OR COUGAR

Mountain lions are found mostly in the Sierra Nevada in the West, including areas of California, Texas, and Idaho. Cougars are found primarily in the Pacific Northwest, Arizona, the desert Southwest, and the Florida Everglades.

Large cats live at altitudes from sea level to 10,000 feet. Large cats tend to avoid human contact, although there have been a few instances in which mountain lions have attacked. According to the U.S. Department of Fish and Game, in the last 100 years only 13 people have been killed by mountain lions. In comparison, lightning has killed 15,000 people, and automobile collisions with deer have killed about 10,000. Still, it is important to be cautious. If you are in cat territory, do not run alone, and make noise when rounding a blind bend in the trail to

avoid surprising one. If you see a large cat:

- Never approach it, especially if cubs are nearby.
- Do not act like prey. Try to appear as large as possible: Wave your arms in the air, grab a stick, open your jacket and spread it wide, and make noise.
- Back away slowly. Do not turn your back to it.
- If attacked, fight back. Convince the animal you are not prey.

WOLVES

There are three types of wolves in the United States: the gray wolf, the Mexican gray, and the red wolf. Although once near extinction, wolves are being reintroduced into the United States in the Southeast, Pacific Northwest, and other areas. Wolves travel in packs of two to fifteen and generally avoid humans. There have been

Digital Imagery © copyright 2001 PhotoDisc, Inc.

Large cats tend to avoid humans.

117

no recorded instances of a wolf killing a human in North America. If you encounter a wolf, do not approach it.

SNAKES

Mention snakes and you are likely to elicit a strong reaction from most people. Whether you feel contempt or hold snakes as a revered symbol, few feel ambiguous toward these creatures. But of all the snakes worldwide, only about 10 percent are poisonous. In the United States, only four types are poisonous, and they are found in every state except Maine, Alaska, and Hawaii. Three of these types are in the family of pit vipers, which include rattlers, copperheads, and cottonmouths, otherwise known as water moccasins. These snakes can be recognized by a small pit between the eye and the nostril, a triangular head, and elliptical-shaped pupils. The other type of poisonous snake is the coral snake. (See Table 5.1.)

Most snakes are shy and avoid human contact. You are most likely to be bitten if you step on a snake or reach into a hole, shrubbery, or other place where visibility is limited. To avoid a snakebite:

■ Watch where you are running. If you see

RECOGNIZING POISONOUS SNAKES

Classification	Markings	Region	Habitat
Rattlesnake	Varies, depending on type. Recognizable by the rattle at the end of the tail.	Many varieties throughout the U.S.	Deserts, mountains, forests, wetlands
Copperhead	Chestnut color. Top of head has a coppery tint.	Eastern U.S. and Midwest	Rocky and mountainous areas
Cottonmouth (water moccasin)	Colors vary. Adults are solid olive, brown, or black.	Southeastern U.S., Illinois, Texas, and Oklahoma	Swamps, lakes, rivers, and ditches
Coral snake	Red-yellow-black band pattern. Brightly colored red and yellow bands touch.	Southern states west to Texas	Wooded areas, swamps, palmetto, and scrub areas

Table 5.1

Clickart ©Broderbund

Leave a least 6 feet between you and a snake.

a snake, slow down or stop and walk around it. Most snakes can strike about half their length. Pass it by no closer than 6 feet.

- If running through tall grass, brush, or rocky areas where visibility is diminished, pound feet heavily to warn nearby snakes. If you are on a narrow trail and a snake will not get out of your way, do not attempt to jump over it. Wait for it to move off the trail.
- If you are jumping over logs or boulders, do so cautiously because snakes often rest in dark, hidden areas.
- If scrambling, watch where you put your hands; never reach into a hole without looking first.

For information on treating snakebites, refer to Chapter 6.

DOGS

Dog bites probably are the most common animal problem on trails. Even domesticated dogs can be unpredictable. According to the U.S. Humane Society, dogs kill about eighteen people a year. You should never assume that a dog will not bite because you have seen it before, because it appears friendly, or just because it is on a leash.

If approaching a dog from behind, keep a safe distance and try not to startle it. A few calming words such as "good dog" can help. If a dog approaches you, do not turn and run. Avert your eyes to avoid direct eye contact and give it plenty of room. If a dog charges you:

- Get something between you and the dog, such as a stick, pack, or jacket.
- If you have pepper spray and have a local law permit for it, use it.
- Often a loud and aggressive "NO" is enough to turn a dog away.
- Fight back. One technique is to put your weaker arm at a 90-degree angle in front of you. The dog will go for that area. With your stronger arm, grab its throat to disable it.

PLANTS

It is important to be aware of potentially harmful plants on the trail. The most common irritants are members of the cashew family: poison ivy, poison oak, and poison sumac.

Stinging nettle and members of the cactus family are also potential hazards.

Perhaps no irritant is as potent as urushiol, the ingredient found in poison ivy, oak, and sumac. As little as $1/4$ of an ounce could create a rash on the entire U.S. population. It is both powerful and persistent:

It has been known to stay potent for up to five years. According to the American Association of Dermatology, up to 85 percent of those who are exposed to urushiol develop a reaction. In this section we will go into detail on how to recognize these plants and avoid exposure; see Chapter 6 for additional first-aid treatment.

COMMON POISONOUS PLANTS

Poison Ivy. (Figure 5.10). Found near lakes and streams in the Midwest and East. This plant usually grows like a woody vine on tree trunks, straggles over the ground like a shrub, or grows upright if unable to attach to something. The leaves usually grow in clusters of three, although the clusters may vary up to nine leaves. The central leaflet has a longer stalk; the other two have almost none. The leaves grow up to 4 inches long. The edges are smooth or toothed. Leaves are reddish in the spring, green in summer, and various shades of yellow, orange, and red in the fall. The plant produces small, greenish or yellow flowers and white berries.

Poison Oak. (Figure 5.11). Found in western states along the Pacific Coast, as well as in the eastern and southeastern United States. This woody, perennial shrub grows up to 6 feet high; vines grow up to 30 feet long. Oaklike leaves are deeply lobed and grow in clusters of three. The leaves can be green or various shades of red and brown. It thrives in shaded areas and near water.

Poison Sumac. (Figure 5.12). Found in the Southern United States. This plant usually grows as a woody, perennial, branching shrub or a small tree. Its leaves

Figure 5.10. Poison Ivy

Figure 5.11. Poison Oak

Figure 5.12. Poison Sumac

are smooth and elliptic and grow in clusters of seven to twelve. It produces small, yellow-white flowers.

PREVENTING EXPOSURE

One of the best ways to prevent exposure to poisonous plants is to keep the skin covered by wearing long pants and long sleeves. Especially if you are running on narrow trails that are not maintained regularly, it may be difficult to avoid touching any of these plants. The powerful irritant bonds to the skin within 15 minutes of contact, and even a quick brush against a leaf can cause infection. Urushiol is found in all parts of the plant, including the root, stem, and leaves. Even in winter, when no leaves are present, contact with the potent toxin is possible. Touching branches and other plants that have come in contact with urushiol can also cause exposure. There are a number of skin products that, if applied to the skin before contact, act as a barrier to prevent the urushiol from bonding to the skin.

Treatment. Treatment for exposure to all three plants is the same. If you think you may have come in contact with one on the trail, try to clean the exposed area immediately with rubbing alcohol (kept in a small towelette in a plastic bag) or soap and cold water. If you do not have access to rubbing alcohol or soap, try to rinse the area immediately in a nearby stream, rubbing vigorously. As soon as you are able, remove and wash your clothes and shower with a mild soap and water. Be careful not to let exposed clothing touch the skin. There are products on the market are specifically designed to remove the harmful oils from the skin and clothing.

CACTI

Many cactus plants have sharp needles, which can pierce a running shoe and cause extreme pain. You may want to find shoes with a thicker upper, such as leather, or wear gaiters to minimize possible intrusion. The most effective way to avoid cactus is to travel slowly in cactus-dense areas. If a needle penetrates the skin, pull it out and cleanse the area.

CHAPTER 6

Jurgen Ankenbrand

Injury Prevention and Treatment

A long trail run can take you miles away from medical care, so a good understanding of basic injury prevention and first aid is essential for all trail runners. Knowledge of these skills will also increase your confidence so you are able to run in more remote areas.

Because trail running is done on a softer, more forgiving surface, there is less risk of certain types of injuries, such as those caused by recurrent impact. But running over uneven ground and obstacles presents its own risks. Wearing proper footwear, warming up, stretching, doing strength training for specific muscle groups, and proprioceptor (balance) training will minimize the risk of many injuries, but knowing how to prevent and treat injuries will make your runs more comfortable and you more confident.

◀◀ ▲   *Softer trail surfaces have unique injury risks.*

Although severe injuries are rare, the possibility makes it wise for someone in your group to carry a cell phone or some other method of communication. It is also essential to have a very good idea of your location so you can tell the rescuers exactly where you are.

Before trail running in a new area, it is prudent to research the climate and plant and animal life indigenous to that area. If you are going for a trail run in Joshua Tree National Park in southern California, for example, you should be aware of the types of cacti growing in the area and the dangerously dry heat of the desert. If your run takes you through the mountains of Idaho in the early spring, you should know that a mountain lion might cross your path. And, obviously, if you are planning to run in the winter in Alaska, you need to know how to prevent hypothermia and frostbite. Again, knowledge is the best prevention:

Know your particular climate and all it has to offer.

COMMON PROBLEMS

BLISTERS

Blisters are one of the most common injuries to trail runners, but they are also one of the easiest to prevent. The first signs of blisters are hot spots, which are sore and reddened areas on the feet; the earlier you treat them, the less likely you are to develop blisters.

Blisters are caused by heat buildup from friction. As the skin heats up, the outer layers separate, and fluid fills in the intervening spaces. The fluid causes more pressure and pain. Trail runners tend to get blisters on the toes and the front of the feet from running downhill and blisters on the Achilles tendons, or heels, from running uphill. Hot spots and blisters can also occur when irritants such as trail dirt or small pebbles get inside the shoe.

Because heat, friction, and moisture combine to form blisters, treating one or all of these conditions will prevent blisters from forming, and this usually starts with proper-fitting shoes and socks. Proper-fitting shoes will prevent your feet from shifting, rubbing, and pinching. Socks with wicking properties or double layers can battle moisture and friction. Make sure the seam of the sock does not wrap around the small toe; some trail runners wear their socks inside out to keep this seam or rib away from the toes.

Powders and lubricants can also combat friction and moisture inside the sock. Powder should be lightly dusted over the feet to avoid caking. If you use lubricant on the heels, toes, or fronts of the feet, reapply it after 1 or 2 hours on a long run, cleansing the area before reapplying if you can.

Many trail runners also use tape to prevent blisters and to reduce existing hot spots. Duct tape and medical tapes are the most widely used; again, your feet should be clean before you apply the tape. If there are any existing blisters, apply a single layer of tape or tissue over the blister. Do not use gauze because it is too abrasive. Tape the affected area, keeping it as smooth as possible; you can use tape adherent to keep the tape attached to the skin, if necessary.

Often, a blister will appear during a run, and if you are a few miles out from the trailhead, you will need to treat it on the trail. You will need four basic ingredients to treat an intact blister on the trail: moleskin, gauze, adhesive, and antibiotic ointment. First, cut a piece of moleskin large enough to surround the blister, with a hole cut out in the center where the blister is. (Adhesive felt or pads can be used in place of moleskin.) Put an antibiotic ointment on the blister. Then cover the area with gauze and adhesive tape. If this does not relieve the pain, you may need to drain the blister and reapply the dressing; however, a blood blister or one that is filled with hazy fluid— indicating infection—should not be drained.

A blood blister occurs when the trauma to the skin is enough to rupture the blood vessels underneath, and blood fills the spaces between the skin layers. These blood blisters are especially susceptible to infection. The blister generally takes several days to heal on its own, but you should stop running until it does so that you do not further tear the outer skin layers, which will delay the healing.

BLACKENED TOENAILS

Blackened toenails are another common problem in trail running. Toenails become bruised when they repeatedly hit the front or the top of the shoe, so blackened toenails are best prevented by shoes with the proper length and adequate width in the toe box. Often black toenails fall off within a few months, and a new nail will grow in. Medical care is not needed unless an infection develops or fluid buildup under the nail is painful.

MUSCLE STRAINS

Because the activity in trail running is constantly changing—from explosive downhill running to slow, powerful, rhythmic uphill running—muscle strains or pulls are common injuries. If your muscle is just sore after a run, the pain will usually subside in 24 hours, but an actual strain is an overuse injury that can lead to further muscle tearing. Because strains are more likely to occur when muscles are cold and tight, you can prevent strains by warming up adequately for 10 minutes followed by stretching.

If you do strain a muscle, the treatment is a combination of icing (described in Chapter 4) and rest. Avoid using the strained muscle while it is still painful. A strained muscle needs rest and healing and should be taken seriously because it will worsen if you continue to run with it. You can also raise the pulled arm or leg muscle above the heart, especially during sleep, to reduce swelling and inflammation.

When the pain has subsided, you can start light activities, but start slowly so as not to reinjure the strained muscle. Besides the pain, other symptoms of a muscle strain are bruising of the skin, impaired movement, and swelling. If you cannot move the affected muscle or limb or if there is external bleeding, you should seek professional medical advice.

SUNBURN

One of the great things about trail running is that it can get you outside for long periods of time in nice, sunny weather. But when you are out on a open trail—wearing a tank top, tee shirt, and short running shorts—sunburn can be a major concern. Sunburn damages skin, causing premature aging, freckling, discoloration, enlarged blood vessels, and skin cancer.

Sunburn is also easily prevented. A sunscreen or sunblock with an SPF of 15 or higher should be used all year long, and during physical activity such as trail running, an SPF of 30 or higher is recommended. Look for a sunscreen that blocks out both UVA and UVB rays. Sunscreens work by reacting with the skin, so you must apply them 20 to 30 minutes before going outdoors. Sunblocks, on the other hand, form a physical barrier between the skin and the sun and work immediately. When using sun protection, look for products that indicate "broad spectrum" because they provide maximum UV protection. Additionally, water-resistant or waterproof products adhere to the skin longer. All products should be applied generously and reapplied at least every 90 minutes of exposure.

People with fair skin may burn after only a few minutes of direct exposure to the sun, but everyone is susceptible. The symptoms of sunburn include redness, a hot or flushed feeling, and soreness. Blisters and itching may occur with severe sunburns after a few days. A severe sunburn over a large area of the body can be accompanied by heat illness, leading to fever and nausea. If this occurs, you should seek medical attention.

If the sunburn is not too severe, you can begin to treat it yourself, and you should start cooling your skin as soon as you can by applying cold compresses for 10 to 15 minutes at a time. You can start this on the trail by drenching a bandana (which you should carry with you in your trail kit) with water from a stream or from your water bottle and gently pressing it to the burned area. If you have ice, you can use a little, but do not leave it directly on the skin for more than 2 minutes.

Once you get off the trail, take a cool or lukewarm bath. A little oatmeal or milk in bath water may also soothe sunburned skin. After bathing, apply moisturizer on the skin while it is still moist to seal in the moisture from the bath water, but use only non-greasy, emollient moisturizer because petroleum jelly or oils may block the pores and actually make the symptoms worse. Do not apply moisturizers or lotions to blisters until they have broken and become dry. Vinegar, baking soda, and harsh soap can irritate and dry out the skin; wash with mild soap or only with water.

To relieve the pain of sunburn, take over-the-counter pain medications such as aspirin, acetaminophen, or ibuprofen. Aloe vera gel can help relieve pain and soothe the skin, and calamine lotion can relieve itching. Finally, because sunburned skin is especially susceptible to dehydration, keep drinking fluids.

SKIN ABRASIONS AND CUTS

Loose rocks or exposed roots on the trail can cause a tumble, resulting in skin abrasions or cuts. When skin is lost, the wound is considered an abrasion, and when the skin is actually gaping open, it is a cut. These openings in the skin break the skin's protective barrier, exposing the soft tissue underneath to infection by bacteria. These minor injuries must be treated properly to avoid infection.

To treat an abrasion or cut, thoroughly clean the abrasion or cut and remove any dirt, gravel, or plant material. On the trail, you can use your water bottle or a stream to irrigate the wound.

For more serious, open cuts, mechanical irrigation is the best method of wound cleaning. To provide this deeper cleaning, try to use something more than water to sterilize the cut. You can carry povidone–iodine solution in your trail pack or first-aid kit. Povidone–iodine pads are also available, or you can make a weak solution by adding an ounce of concentrated povidone–iodine solution to a liter of your cleanest water along with a teaspoon of salt. (Salt increases the effectiveness of the antiseptic solution.) Shake the mixture and wait 5 minutes to allow the iodine to disinfect the water completely. Forcefully irrigate the cut by using a syringe held 2 to 4 inches above the area or putting the solution in a plastic bag with a small hole cut in one corner and then squeezing the bag. You can also melt a pinhole in the lid of one of your water bottles and use this for forceful irrigation.

Scrapes are better treated by scrubbing. To scrub a scrape, use a small scrub brush or cloth, such as a bandana, to scrub the area. Use regular soap or an antibacterial cleanser from your kit, if available. Otherwise, use clean, fresh water. If you clean the area with soap, follow with a very thorough irrigation using clean water. Dry the area thoroughly with a clean or sterile gauze sponge.

If the cut is gaping, apply some closure strips (butterfly bandages) once it is clean and dry. Apply an antibiotic ointment to the abrasion or cut and cover the entire area with a nonstick bandage. A bandage is important because it provides a moist environment, which aids healing, protects the area from more damage by bumping or scraping, and limits movement that can impair healing. Change the bandage every 24 to 48 hours or whenever it becomes wet or very soiled. Continue using a bandage and ointment until the wound is completely healed from the inside out. You should discourage scab formation because it impairs oxygen delivery to the wound, delaying healing. Scabs also tend to crack

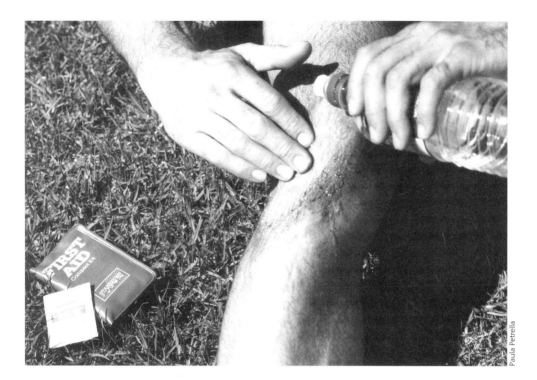

Paula Petrella

Thoroughly clean abrasions and remove debris.

open easily and bleed and will leave a worse scar.

MUSCLE CRAMPS

A muscle cramp occurs when a muscle remains contracted for a minute or more before finally relaxing. This occurs when lactic acid and other byproducts of metabolism accumulate in the muscle.

If a muscle cramp occurs while you are on the trail, gently stretch the offending muscle or try gentle massage, beginning at the edge of the cramp and moving toward the center, squeezing the muscle gently to relieve the cramp. You may have to slow your pace or walk to see whether the cramp resolves.

If the muscle continues to cramp, complete your run at a walk or very slow jog to avoid a serious injury to the muscle. As soon as possible, put an ice pack on the cramping muscle. After the first 24 hours, you can immerse the cramping area in warm water and try to massage the muscle while stretching it.

Generally, these cramps subside in less

than 24 hours. If the muscle remains sore the next day, however, the discomfort can indicate something more serious, and you should cut back on your training schedule for several days. Trainers recommend decreasing your distance by about 30 percent until the pain resolves.

Cramps accompanied by dizziness or disorientation can indicate dehydration or early heat stroke. Get out of the sun immediately and sit or lie down in the shade. Sip water slowly. Cramping in the chest, shoulders, or arms can be a sign of a heart attack. Sit or lie down in the shade and have one of your running partners immediately go for help.

MINOR AND MAJOR INJURIES

SPRAINS

Sprains are a more severe form of strain. Ankle sprains are the most common form of minor injury for trail runners. And the most common type of ankle sprain is an inversion sprain, which happens when the foot is forced to roll to the outside rather than the inside, as it does with normal pronation. The inversion sprain's opposite is called an eversion sprain, caused when the ankle rolls too far to the inside.

Ankle sprains usually occur when the running surface is uneven and the ground's ruts and holes are hidden, making the hazards more difficult to see. Proceed slowly on rough, potholed terrain and through tall grass.

Because ankle sprains can cause other injuries, including tears in the joint capsule or even fractures, they must be treated right away. The first treatment for a sprained ankle is rest, ice, compression, and elevation (RICE). If a sprain occurs on the trail, limp back carefully to your car, putting as little weight as possible on the injured ankle. As soon as possible, elevate the injured leg and apply ice packs to the ankle. You should see a physician as soon as possible because X-rays usually are needed to rule out a fracture. Your doctor may also prescribe an ankle brace, physical therapy, casting, or surgery, depending on the seriousness of the injury.

TORN LIGAMENTS

Ligaments are strong strips of connective tissue found in and near joints. For trail runners, knees and ankles may be particularly susceptible to torn ligaments because these parts bear the stresses from uneven ground.

The knee has four ligaments: one on each side of the knee and two within the joint itself. These ligaments can be stretched or sprained, or partially or completely torn. A ligament tear causes bleeding inside the joint, causing pain and making the joint unable to bear any weight. Severe forces generally cause tears, but some tears can be caused by more moderate forces. The anterior cruciate ligament in the knee joint, for example, can be torn by the force of landing after a jump. Some athletes suffer from what are known as chronic ligament tears, and their ligaments

EXERCISES TO HELP PREVENT ANKLE SPRAINS

- **Band exercises:** With your knees, feet, and ankles together, tie a rubber exercise band loosely around your feet. Pull your feet apart, then relax. Repeat ten times. Next, tie the band around the feet with your ankles crossed. Push one foot out to the side and relax. Repeat with the other foot, then relax. Repeat ten times.
- **Alphabet writing:** Sitting in a chair, with one leg extended in front of you, use your big toe as a pen to write the alphabet in the air, moving your ankle to form the letters. Repeat three times with each foot.

may give way during an activity in which there is a specific movement that is repeated, such as moving to the side (as in skiing) or landing after a jump (as in basketball). These side-to-side and landing movements are also encountered in trail running. Over a period of time, chronic tears can lead to other damage to the knee menisci and cartilage, eventually leading to osteoarthritis.

Treatment for a sprain or partial tear of a knee ligament may require a brace or cast for four to six weeks. Treat a chronic tear by consistently wearing a brace to stabilize the knee. An acute complete tear, however, requires surgery in which the torn ligaments are sewn back together, followed by four to six weeks in a cast. After such an injury, return to full trail running may take nine months to a year. As always, if you feel pain or hear a popping sound in a joint, stop running and apply ice followed by compression and elevation.

Three ligaments stabilize the ankle joint. A bad sprain—grade three or third degree sprain—in the ankle generally means that a ligament has been torn. In trail running,

this injury typically occurs from jumping, stepping on uneven ground, or sharp direction changes. Other risk factors for a torn ankle ligament—besides uneven ground—are previous untreated ankle injuries, being overweight, or wearing poorly fitted or worn-out shoes.

Generally, a severe ankle sprain and ligament tear is accompanied by massive swelling, severe tenderness and joint instability. Walking may not be possible and surgery may be necessary. But again, the most important first step with a potential ankle injury is to stop running, apply ice, and elevate the ankle as soon as possible with compression.

FRACTURES

A severe sprain can be difficult to differentiate from a fracture, but dislocations and fractures are serious injuries that necessitate trained medical advice and treatment. If you fracture one of the leg bones or dislocate a hip, you may not be able to get up from where you have fallen. If you can, apply ice as soon as possible to minimize swelling, and send for help.

More common for runners are stress fractures. These occur when the bone breaks down faster than it is rebuilt. Usually the first sign of a stress fracture is a tenderness to the touch over the bone. Stop running until the tenderness resolves. If it does not resolve after one week, seek medical advice to rule out a stress fracture.

HEAD INJURIES

Head injuries and neurological problems are uncommon for trail runners, but they can occur if you fall while running. If there is a possibility of a neck injury, do not attempt to move. Use compresses on any areas that are bleeding, but do not attempt to move from the position in which you have landed. Call for emergency services immediately.

Severe bleeding and other vascular problems can also result from head injuries. If you sustain an injury that bleeds profusely, follow the instructions as noted for abrasions and cuts and call for assistance.

Initially apply pressure in the form of compression to the wound. Hold the pressure tightly for 5 minutes. If the bleeding has stopped, try to clean and dress the wound. If the bleeding continues, keep applying pressure until the bleeding stops. Once the bleeding stops, apply a butterfly bandage to close the edges of the wound and prevent further bleeding; dress the wound tightly with a pressure dressing. Seek medical attention immediately. If the wound continues to bleed, you may not be able to move from your location and you will have to call for emergency assistance.

CAR KIT LIST

In addition to the basic first-aid equipment you carry with you on the trail, you should keep a more extensive first-aid kit in your car. You can buy a kit or assemble your own that contains these items:

- Oral rehydration salt packets for treating diarrhea and dehydration
- Irrigation syringe for wound cleansing
- Nonadherent gauze pads or second-skin dressings, adhesive pads, and wound closure strips
- Tincture of benzoin to help tape and bandages adhere to sweaty and dirty skin
- Sterile pads or sterile gauze sticks
- Antibiotic ointment
- Acetaminophen for pain reduction, ibuprofen for inflammation reduction
- Topical analgesics for treating mild allergic reactions
- Epinephrine for serious allergies

ENVIRONMENT-RELATED ILLNESS

HYPOTHERMIA AND FROSTBITE

Hypothermia is a condition that occurs when the body's temperature falls below 96 degrees Fahrenheit. Left untreated, it can lead to a loss of consciousness, cardiac arrest, and death. Hypothermia is most often associated with cold temperatures between 30 and 50 degrees Fahrenheit, but it can also occur in mild temperatures if you become wet and exhausted. The first signs of hypothermia are shivering, uncoordinated movements, vague or slurred speech, drowsiness, weakness, and loss of consciousness. If you think you or someone you are with may be hypothermic, get help as soon as possible. While waiting for the medical help, start the following treatments.

Get the victim to shelter. If his or her clothes are wet, change them. Warm the victim by covering the head and neck. Along with any blankets or clothing that is available, use your own body heat to help warm the victim. If they are available, you can also place warm compresses next to the victim, but do not use direct heat, such as an electric blanket. If the victim is conscious, give him or her sips of warm, sweetened water.

Because loss of consciousness can occur, it is also important to check the victim's airway, breathing, and circulation (ABCs). Lay the victim on his or her back and lift the chin to open the airway. Bring your ear close to the victim's mouth to see whether he or she is breathing. Then check the neck artery for a pulse; because hypothermia victims often have very weak, slow pulses, spend extra time checking for a pulse. If there is no breathing, begin artificial respiration; if there is no breathing and no pulse, begin cardiopulmonary resuscitation if you are certified.

Frostbite is caused by long exposure to cold. Superficial frostbite may damage only the outer layer of skin, but severe frostbite affects the deep tissues and may result in gangrene. The toes, ears, and tip of the nose are especially vulnerable to frostbite. Signs of frostbite include numb, cold skin; skin that turns blue or white or looks blackened and becomes hard, waxy, and frozen; and loss of function in the frozen area. Initially, there is no sensation of pain, but pain usually occurs when the blood seeps back into the tissues after a few hours. If the skin turns purple or black as the blood seeps back in, get to an emergency facility immediately.

Seek shelter while awaiting medical help or treating frostbite. Remove any tight clothing or jewelry. Warm the affected area gradually, and do not rub the injured tissue. The best treatment for frostbitten hands or feet is to place them in a bowl of water no hotter than 105 degrees Fahrenheit for 20 minutes, adding warm water as it cools. You can also soak a cotton cloth in warm water and place it on the frostbitten area for 30 minutes, resoaking the cloth to keep it warm. If warm water is not available, use body warmth, blankets, or newspapers to warm the skin. Once the damaged skin is soft and warm and the feeling and color return, dry the skin and place a clean, dry cloth over it. Place clean, dry cloths between frostbitten fingers, and wrap more dry cloths around the area to keep it warm.

To avoid frostbite during cold weather, clothing should be well-fitting, warm, and wind resistant. Tight shoes, socks, or gloves diminish circulation and are dangerous to the extremities. People with diabetes or other circulatory problems are at more risk for developing frostbite.

TRENCH FOOT

Trench foot, often called immersion foot, is nerve and muscle damage resulting from prolonged exposure to moisture or cold but without ice formation (frostbite) in the cells of the affected area. Trench foot occurs in three phases. Initially the foot is cold to the touch, slightly swollen and discolored, numb, and tender, similar to the "pins and needles" sensation when a limb that has fallen asleep is waking up. At this point, when the foot is rewarmed the damaged area appears red and may remain sore for several days.

The second phase occurs when the cells of the foot have become damaged by the lack of circulation, and the foot swells with tingling pain. Upon rewarming, blisters form and may progress to ulcers, and gangrene can result from severe cases.

The third lasts weeks to months and occurs when the swelling subsides and the foot again appears normal but has an increased sensitivity to cold, itching, and pain. The foot can be more susceptible to cold injury in the future.

If you think you may have trench foot, stop and dry the foot, elevate it above the heart, and rewarm with skin-to-skin contact. Do not rub the foot or place it near a strong heat source. Take anti-inflammatory drugs such as ibuprofen or aspirin. It takes 24 to 48 hours before the full extent of the damage is apparent.

Trench foot can be caused by a variety of conditions: poor nutrition, dehydration, wet socks, inadequate clothing, and constriction in the feet by socks or shoes that are too tight. Keeping the feet dry and comfortable can prevent trench foot. Keep a dry pair of extra socks in your pack in a plastic bag, and make sure your shoes fit properly.

HEAT ILLNESS

Hot temperatures and high humidity can cause serious illnesses. Whether you are indoors or outdoors in direct sunlight, you should be aware of the conditions and symptoms of heat cramps, heat exhaustion, and heat stroke. These conditions occur when intense heat or humidity reduces the body's ability to control its temperature; the body cannot produce enough sweat or the sweat is not evaporating fast enough to cool the body. This happens when you have not ingested enough fluids to make sweat or when the humidity rises and it is difficult for sweat to evaporate to dissipate the heat. (See Table 6.1.) Your core body temperature can rise to dangerous levels, which can result in heat cramps, heat exhaustion, heat stroke, and death.

Heat cramps usually are the first signs of trouble. These are muscle cramps or spasms (twitching), mostly in the arms, legs, or stomach. These cramps occur during exercise or overexertion in the heat, and they are caused by a loss of fluid and minerals, especially salt and potassium. These cramps may be painful, but they are not dangerous in themselves. However, ignoring heat cramps can lead to heat exhaustion, which occurs when the body's temperature regulation mechanisms are overtaxed and on their way to shutting down.

Simply exercising in the heat may cause heat cramps, but more serious exhaustion stems from a combination of extreme heat and inadequate fluid consumption. You may still sweat profusely, but if heat exhaustion is not treated, the sweating will stop as the cooling system shuts down. Symptoms of heat exhaustion include feeling dizzy, weak, faint, cold, and clammy. You may also develop a headache and nausea, and with more severe cases you can develop dizziness, fainting, vomiting, rapid breathing, and lack of coordination. If you have heat exhaustion and continue to push yourself, you will develop heat stroke, which is a medical emergency and can lead to death.

In heat stroke your body's cooling mechanisms completely shut down. If you

Temperature and Heat Illness

Temp	Relative Humidity							
	30%	40%	50%	60%	70%	80%	90%	100%
100	104	110	120	132	144	157	170	—
95	96	101	107	114	124	136	150	166
90	90	93	96	100	106	113	122	133
85	84	86	88	90	93	97	102	108
80	78	79	81	82	85	86	88	91
75	73	74	75	76	77	78	79	80
70	67	68	69	70	70	71	71	72

☐ Heat stroke possible   ☐ Heat exhaustion likely, heat stroke possible   ☐ Heat stroke likely

Table 6.1

faint, vomit, or cannot drink water, you need to get immediate medical care because you probably have heat stroke. Other symptoms include disorientation, lack of perspiration, vomiting, unconsciousness, and high body temperature (from 103 to 108 degrees Fahrenheit).

The best treatment for heat illness is prevention: Drink plenty of water, whether you are thirsty or not. (Sports drinks that contain sugar may not be absorbed as quickly as water.) The first few weeks of hot weather are the most dangerous. Cut back on your exercise routine by 25 percent and slowly build back up to your usual level in a week. Exercise during the coolest times of the day, before 10 A.M. or after 6 P.M. Make your workouts easier on particularly hot or humid days. Wear light-colored clothing to reflect sunlight.

If you start developing symptoms, treat them before they escalate. If you feel heat cramps, stop exercising and get out of the heat. Treat these cramps by stretching and massaging the muscles and drinking plenty of fluids.

If you have heat exhaustion, get to shelter—preferably someplace with air conditioning or a fan—or rest in the shade and fan yourself or have someone fan you. Apply cold compresses and drink water slowly.

If the condition has escalated to a heat stroke, call for emergency services immediately and try to cool down by fanning yourself, drenching your clothes in cool water (or even pouring cool water over yourself), and applying cold packs.

DEHYDRATION AND HYPONATREMIA

Dehydration can lead to serious heat illness. You can prevent dehydration by drinking plenty of water before, during, and after your workouts. A more thorough discussion of dehydration is provided in Chapter 2.

Dehydration can lead to lowered endurance, impaired equilibrium, reduced mental activity, and impaired ability to regulate the body temperature. Muscle cramps can occur during runs and may be a sign of dehydration. Muscle cramps caused by dehydration may also herald the onset of hyponatremia (also called water intoxication), which is a shortage of sodium in the blood. It occurs when you sweat excessively, losing salt, and then drink excessive amounts of water, which dilutes the remaining sodium in the blood. It is more likely to occur in hot, humid weather and among runners who are out on the course for long periods of time, generally more than 4 hours. Endurance athletes, such as trail runners who do ultra-marathons, are especially vulnerable because of the length of these events.

The early warning signs of hyponatremia are similar to those of dehydration: fatigue, weakness, muscle cramping, dizziness, confusion, and nausea. At this point, many runners think they need to drink more water, which only aggravates the problem and can lead to vomiting, fainting, seizures, coma, and even death. These symptoms tend to occur late in a run or even afterward. At the first signs of muscle cramping, nausea, or disorientation, drink a sports drink that contains sodium or eat salty foods. If the symptoms worsen, seek medical treatment immediately.

To prevent hyponatremia, use a sports drink with sodium, instead of water, to replace fluid loss during and after a race. You can add salt to your food in the days before your long runs or races. Foods that can provide additional sodium include pretzels, dill pickles, tomato juice, and chicken noodle soup. Increase your salt intake by 10 to 25 grams per day for several days before an event. Also, during the last half of a race or long run, you can eat salted pretzels. Try to avoid nonsteroidal anti-inflammatory drugs such as aspirin, ibuprofen, and naproxen sodium before or during a race or long run. A safer drug to use for pain relief during these runs is acetaminophen.

ALTITUDE SICKNESS

The symptoms of altitude or mountain sickness develop when you ascend to higher elevations and the body responds to the reduced oxygen content at this elevation. Most people have no problems up to 8,000 feet in elevation, but above 10,000 feet, many experience some mild symptoms of Acute Mountain Sickness (AMS). Symptoms include headache, sleeplessness, nausea, shortness of breath, fatigue, dizziness, and loss of appetite. The only cure for mountain sickness is descent: once you come down from that elevation, you will begin to feel better almost immediately.

Severe AMS can be life threatening. To prevent altitude sickness on a long or multiday run, ascend slowly over 2 to 3 days to give your body time to adjust, or descend to below 8,000 feet to sleep or for a few hours each day. If you cannot do either of these things, then for the first few days take it easy, drink a lot of water, and limit caffeine and alcohol. You can take aspirin or acetaminophen for a headache, but do not take sleeping pills. The prescription medication acetazolamide often is used to prevent altitude sickness.

ANIMAL-RELATED HEALTH PROBLEMS

One of the joys of trail running is animal sightings: They remind you that you are out in nature, far from city life. However, animals present their own hazards, from simple mosquito bites to more dangerous encounters with poisonous creatures. Be aware of the animal life in your area, and if you are running in a new area, do a little research on its inhabitants.

SNAKEBITES

Rattlesnakes, copperheads, and water moccasins are known as mild pit vipers, and a bite from one of these snakes will result in black and blue skin, tenderness or swelling, or blistering. The actual danger from this venom depends on the size, health, emotional stability, and age of the victim. It also depends on whether he or she is allergic to the venom, the location of the bite (more dangerous near vital organs), how deep the fangs went, how much venom was injected, how afraid the snake was, the species and size of the snake, and the first aid provided. The following treatment guidelines have been developed primarily for pit viper bites but should be followed for all snakebites.

Remain calm and rest, with the bitten extremity immobilized and kept lower than the heart. Remove anything that may constrict the area, such as rings and watches, in case swelling occurs. Wash the wound and monitor the swelling by measuring the area, if possible. Get medical help as soon as possible. You can walk slowly if you feel stable. If you are not able to get medical help within 30 minutes, use mechanical extraction from a snakebite kit. Do not cut the wound and do not suck the venom. Avoid the use of painkillers, ice, immersion, and cold-water compresses, and do not apply a tourniquet.

SPIDERS AND SCORPIONS

Almost all spiders carry venom, but only a few species have a bite harmful to humans. Most spider bites are painless.

The most venomous spider in the United States is the black widow, which has been found in every state except Alaska. Only the female is dangerous; she is easily identifiable by the red hourglass shape on her abdomen. The bite of the black widow is rarely felt, but symptoms occur within 10 to 60 minutes, beginning with pain, anxiety, and severe muscle cramping.

If you suspect a spider bite, remain calm. If you can find the site of the bite, wash it

thoroughly and apply povidone–iodine solution. Ice applied to spider bites will reduce pain, slow the spread of the venom, and allow the body to more easily break down the venom. Antivenom is available, and you should seek medical attention to receive it.

Although black widow spiders are the most poisonous, the most common spider bite in the United States is from the brown recluse spider. This spider generally is a pale brown to reddish color with slender legs that are 2 to 3 centimeters long. It is found primarily in dark and dry places in the South and southern Midwest. Brown recluse spiders attack more readily in warmer weather and usually at night, but only when disturbed. They have dull fangs and inflict their bites on tender areas. A painful blister develops within 5 hours, with a bluish circle around the blister and a red circle beyond that. This bull's-eye lesion is characteristic.

As with other spider bites, remain calm, wash the wound, and apply a cold compress. Seek medical attention if you develop a fever, chills, a rash, or an ulcer at the site of the bite. You can avoid almost all contact with dangerous spiders by looking before you put your hands in dark places.

Like most spiders, scorpions hide by day and move around at night. A scorpion sting tends to be more painful than a spider bite. The only species that is known to cause death in humans is the *Centruroides,* which is found only in Mexico and the extreme southwestern United States. First aid, as with spider bites, includes remaining calm and still, and cooling and cleaning the wound. Antitoxins are available.

BEES, TICKS, MOSQUITOES, AND FLIES

Bee, mosquito, tick, and black fly bites can all cause painful irritations and possibly more serious diseases. The most effective insect repellents contain *DEET, (N,N-diethyl-metatoluamide)*, but there are also natural repellents for those who want to avoid the toxins in DEET. An application of a 30- to 50-percent DEET product lasts 4 to 6 hours and is considered safer than repeated applications of lower dosages of DEET products. Natural formulations of insect repellents, such as citronella products, work for 2 to 4 hours and generally do not repel ticks and bees.

Mosquito and black fly bites usually cause only irritation. Itching can be minimized by applying ice or cold compresses or by using a topical analgesic. Mosquito or fly stings rarely cause serious allergic reactions, but if severe swelling occurs, treat in the same way as a bee sting allergy.

Hornets, bees, wasps, and yellow jackets are attracted to black, yellow, red, and blue. To avoid attracting their attention, wear light-colored clothing and refrain from wearing perfume or cologne. Also, waving wildly or swatting at the insects will anger them, making them more likely to bite or sting.

If you are stung, cool the area with cold compresses. If the stinger is still in place, remove it by scraping the surface of the area. Grasping the stinger will cause injection of more venom. Use a topical analgesic for mild swelling and itching. If a severe reaction occurs, such as marked swelling, difficulty breathing, or rapid heartbeat, seek immediate medical attention. All complete first-aid kits include epinephrine for bee sting allergies.

Ticks are most active during the breeding months of May through July. Tick bites themselves may be only mildly irritating, but they can carry other serious diseases such as Lyme disease and Rocky Mountain spotted fever.

Early detection is one of the best ways to prevent tick problems. After every run, especially a run through dense brush or where the body has come into contact with the ends of branches and shrubbery, check for ticks. Because ticks attach themselves to your body and drain blood, preferably from dark, moist areas and crevices, they gravitate toward areas in the socks, under the armpits, between the legs, or in the stomach area.

If you find a tick on your body, try to remove it by slowly pulling the tick away from your skin without twisting or jerking, grasping as close as possible to the head with your fingers or with a pair of tweezers from your kit. If you cannot remove the tick by pulling, apply permethrin (insecticidal repellent) on a cotton swab and dab it directly on the tick, wait 15 minutes, and try pulling again. Check the site after removing the tick to make sure no part of the tick remains. Wash the area, and then apply a povidone–iodine solution. Save the tick, if possible, by placing it in a plastic bag with some alcohol or an alcohol swab. If you develop disease symptoms at a later date, the tick will be used to identify the illness.

If you know you will be trail running in a tick-infested area (the northeastern United States has the biggest tick and Lyme disease problem, although ticks are found in many states), apply DEET insect repellents directly to the skin, and also apply permethrin repellent directly to your clothing. Permethrin products repel and kill mosquitoes and ticks for two weeks and through two launderings.

CHIGGERS

Chiggers, found primarily in the southeastern United States, are the larvae of the harvest mite. The eight-legged adult harvest mites are bright red and look like small, velvety red spiders. The tiny, six-legged larval chigger crawls onto feet or legs and moves about until it reaches a place such as ankles, under socks, or the waistline. Bites from the tiny larval chigger mites are not a serious health concern, but the irritation they cause can last several weeks.

Chiggers pierce the skin and inject a fluid that causes tissues to be inflamed; each bite has a characteristic red welt with a hard, white center. Severe itching and dermatitis usually accompany chigger bites. After becoming fully fed,

Paula Petrella

Check for ticks after any run through dense vegetation.

the chigger drops from its host.

Because several hours elapse before chiggers settle down to bite, bathing soon after exposure to chigger-infested areas may wash chiggers off your body and prevent feeding. Clothing also should be washed to prevent reinfestation.

The most suitable breeding areas for chigger mites are among weeds and thick vegetation where there is an abundance of moisture and shade. Chiggers become most active in June. DEET will make your body less attractive for chigger feeding. For maximum effectiveness, apply repellents to your shoes, socks, pant cuffs, ankles, legs, and waist. Over-the-counter lotions and ointments may relieve itching of chigger bites.

RABIES

Rabies is very unusual in the United States: Only thirty-six cases have been reported in the United States since 1980, and 33 percent of these cases were acquired abroad in rabies-endemic countries. If you are going to be trail running in a country in which rabies in wildlife is common, you should discuss pre-exposure prophylaxis with your physician. If you are trail running in the United States or in a country with good medical access, rabies vaccine and rabies immune globulin are readily available, and no special precautions are needed.

If an animal such as a bat or wild dog bites you, try to capture it and take it to a medical facility to determine whether it is rabid. If you cannot regain the animal, still seek medical attention to determine whether you should have rabies vaccine or immune globulin.

POISONOUS AND DANGEROUS PLANTS

Urushiol is the ingredient in plants that makes them poisonous and is described in detail in Chapter 5. Some cacti have a similar poison in their stingers. Symptoms of a reaction to the poison are itching, burning, redness, blisters, and swelling.

On the trail, you should treat contact with a poisonous plant much as you would a cut or a scrape. Wash the area as best you can with a water bottle, in a stream, or with povidone–iodine solution. You can also apply ice, but most importantly, avoid scratching the area because this will spread toxin along the skin to other areas. An analgesic tablet will help with the itching. Once you arrive back at your car, apply a mild antihistamine cream or mild steroid cream from your full first-aid kit to help relieve the itching.

Unless you ingest the plant, fatalities from plant poisonings are extremely rare. The worst outcome usually is severe discomfort, although a skin infection can develop if the skin breaks and the area is not kept clean. Once you return home, contact your local poison control center for additional information; a visit to the emergency room is rarely necessary.

CHAPTER 7

Jurgen Ankenbrand

Bringing It to the Next Level: Ultrarunning

"It is like living a lifetime condensed into a matter of hours. There is joy and suffering, optimism and fear, elation and sadness. When you cross the finish line, there is the satisfaction of accomplishing what you set out to do without the obligation of dying when it comes to an end."

Ultralist message, author unknown

Ultramarathons have been around almost as long as marathons. Despite their obscurity until the last 30 years, their popularity is growing quickly. In 1977, there were only about thirty. Now, according to Kevin Setnes, ultrarunning coach, competitor, and cochair of the Mountain Ultra Trail Council, more

◀◀ ▲ *Ultrarunning provides the ultimate trail experience.*

than 350 trail ultras are held in the United States annually.

An ultrarun or ultrarace is defined as any run over the 26.2-mile marathon distance. Ultramarathons usually are in distances of 50 kilometers (31 miles), 50 miles, 100 kilometers (62 miles), 100 miles, and longer distances, such as the Badwater 135-mile race and the multiday Marathon Des Sables. The longest certified run is a 1,300-mile run, in which runners circle around a 1-mile loop track 1,300 times. Some ultramarathons are run over a set time period, such as 24, 48, or 72 hours, in which runners attempt the greatest possible distance in the time allotted.

Many ultraraces are held on trails and fire roads and traverse snow and ice, sand, mud, and scree in a single event; these varying trail conditions are part of what attracts ultrarunners. Trail ultras often include the additional challenges of altitude gains and losses, more aggressive terrain, and night running.

Because most ultras are held in natural areas not made to handle the level of foot traffic of usual road races, they are often limited to a few hundred entrants. Compare this to their marathon counterparts, which often have up to 20,000 entrants, and you can see how this environment creates a camaraderie and intimacy not found in road races. Ultrarunners all share a great love of trail running. Shannon Farrar-Griefer, who has competed in more than thirty ultras, comments, "In a 50- or 100-mile run, you're struggling out there a lot of the time. So we help each other. We're sharing something in common; we all share the passion of running."

Ultraruns are a great opportunity to be challenged on trails. Quite often in ultra-racing, the accomplishment of finishing is a victory in itself.

YOUR FIRST 50K

Although the 50k technically is an ultrarun distance, it has more in common with the marathon than with a 50- or 100-mile race. Therefore, few adjustments are needed in the training program to make the transition from marathon to 50k. One helpful adjustment would be to change the length of your longest run by adding 4 to 8 miles. For example, if the longest run in your marathon training program is 22 miles, adjust that run to 26 to 28 miles.

You should run your first 50k with a goal of finishing at a comfortable pace. Once you have experienced the distance, you can set time goals. Many ultrarunners feel better after a 50k than after a hard-run marathon because the softer trail surface puts less stress on the musculoskeletal system. Additionally, the varied terrain on trails helps use muscles in varied ways, thus preventing the muscles from being overtaxed with repetitive motion.

TRAINING FOR A 50-MILER

Training for an ultrarun involves the same principles as a marathon or shorter-distance training program. Periodization (which is

explained in Chapter 3), building up to the long run, alternating hard and easy workouts, tapering, warm-ups, stretching, and good nutrition are all standard elements of training that apply to shorter distances and ultrarunning alike. However, there are key differences, which we discuss in this chapter.

As with shorter road distances, no single program works for everyone. Factors such as age, physical condition, and genetic ability all determine individual responses to training intensity and mileage limits. Some runners who regularly compete in ultras comfortably run more than 100 miles per

View from the Leona Divide 50 mile race

Jurgen Ankenbrand

week, whereas others can handle only 40 miles per week. Despite these differences, they all have one thing in common: building up to the long run. Long runs prepare the endocrine system for the additional stresses put on the body and familiarize the muscles and the mind with endurance running.

You should include at least two or three long runs of 25 to 35 miles in your training program. The runs should be two or three weeks apart to give the body time to recover. The other weeks, you should run a medium distance. Do your last long run at least three weeks before a 50-mile race. Although your weekly mileage need not increase, if you do add miles, buildup should be no more than 10 percent more per week.

One of the keys to success in ultra-running is to duplicate the actual race conditions as much as possible while training. The more you mimic race conditions in training, the more prepared you will be, mentally and physically. This includes running on trail surfaces similar to the course, running in similar weather, ingesting food and water on the run, using the same equipment (such as your hydration system), and practicing varying paces.

In training for a trail ultra, split your weekly mileage between trail and road running. Trail running builds muscle strength, but if it is done exclusively your body will not increase in speed because leg turnover rate on trails is usually slower. Alternating road and trail running builds up speed and leg strength.

One of the big differences between an ultrarun and a marathon is that in an ultra you are likely to walk. There are various methods for taking walk breaks, including those gauged by trail conditions, time, or heart rate, or simply by feel. Many choose to walk the uphills and run the flats and the downhills. Two common time systems are the 25/5 (run for 25 minutes, then walk for 5) and the 5/1 (run for 5 minutes, then walk 1). The 25/5 method allows the heart rate to slow down, thus allowing the body to digest the necessary food and water. Other runners simply run when they can and walk when they cannot. You will determine what system works for you by practicing and listening to your own body.

In training for an ultrarun, you should practice walking fast. Getting your legs used to walking with long, fast strides will prevent you from taking it too slow on walking breaks. A strong walker can often pass a slower runner on the uphill portions of a race. You should also practice running slowly. This is useful at the end of a 50- or 100-miler when your body is tired but you still want to run rather than walk.

Another key difference in long races is the importance of nutrition and hydration. This is crucial in an ultrarun, where you will be on the trail for an average of ten hours in a 50-miler. In a 100-mile race, you will burn approximately 10,000 calories. If you are not used to eating on the run, practice in training runs to see what foods work for you. In 50- and 100-mile races, many runners opt for normal foods consumed in their daily diets, such as potatoes, sandwiches, soups, and fruits, rather relying solely on gels and bars. Ingesting sufficient quantities of carbohydrates, potassium, sodium, and water (as described in Chapters 2 and 3) is critical to your health and performance.

It is also important to take good care of your feet. You may be able to hobble through with a blister at the latter stages of a marathon, but the length of an ultrarun demands that you take immediate action to prevent blisters and chafing, thus preventing a miserable long run. You should be well informed about blister and foot care (see Chapter 6) and take care of your feet the moment you feel a problem arising.

TRAINING FOR THE 100-MILER

Running 100 miles might seem impossible, but it is an exciting challenge. Karl King, experienced ultrarunner, said, "When my longest run was 13 miles, a marathon seemed nearly impossible. When my longest run was 26 miles, 50 miles seemed nearly impossible. When my longest run was 50 miles, 100 miles seemed nearly impossible. When my longest run was 100 miles, 50 miles seemed like a nice, long training run."

Running 100 miles takes additional mental fortitude. Coach Kevin Setnes observes that 100 miles is not just double a 50-mile race. It often takes two and a half to three times as long to complete. It also takes a committed resolve to move forward despite exhaustion, muscle fatigue, and signals in your brain that tell you to stop. He recommends building up your long run to two or three runs per week of 30 to 40 miles to train the mind and body to adapt.

Running at Night

Running 100 miles entails running at night. Being able to stay awake and coherent is part of the challenge. A week before the event, pay special attention to getting enough sleep. Often the excitement of the race keeps runners awake the night before. Although some runners take short naps during a 100-mile race, many opt not to. In doing so it is easy to miss a cutoff time, get too stiff to want to continue, or sleep too long.

Many use caffeine and sugar to stay awake. Ultrarunner Norm Yarger uses this method: "I give up caffeine two weeks prior to a 100, and continue to abstain in the race. About 10 P.M., I start drinking it. This carries me through the night." Ultrarunner Matt Mahoney carefully measures his caffeine intake by ingesting 100 milligrams, which is the equivalent to one cup of coffee or two sodas, about every three hours beginning at 10 P.M. Most runners feel a surge of energy at daybreak, regardless of caffeine intake or naps.

Eyestrain can contribute to fatigue during a race and running at night can contribute to eyestrain. Running at night is a very different experience because visibility is limited, which results in a slower pace. In training, try a nighttime or all-night run on the trail in order to acclimate. You should practice with various headlamps and flashlights at different intensities to see what works best and also practice without artificial light. You will probably run both with and without artificial light during a 100-mile race. Running without artificial light allows a wider range of vision on the trail; artificial lights can create a sort of tunnel vision, illuminating one spot and obscuring the surrounding areas. Eyes that are used to the darkness can also spot small obstacles and trail markers. Conversely, too little light causes eyestrain.

When using a headlamp, bring a handheld flashlight to illuminate below. This prevents having to turn your head in an awkward position. It is best to run with a few friends. Running at night during the race may be easier than during training because of the added excitement and purpose of the race.

What About the Wall?

Nick Marshall, author of *The Complete Marathoner,* points out that many people think the body can comfortably handle only 20 miles before reaching a state of exhaustion. So, many believe that a longer distance is incomprehensible. He explains, "Depletion sets in [at 20 miles] in a hard effort only because [the runner] is approaching the finish and has apportioned his energy accordingly." In other words, if you have trained for a marathon, you have trained your body to comfortably handle 20 miles and are fit to push the extra 6 miles to finish. Most people hit the wall at 20 miles because that is the distance they have

trained their bodies to handle comfortably. If you train your body to go longer, it will.

RACE STRATEGY

Your goal in your first ultrarun should be to finish at a conservative pace, with less concern for finishing time. Be aware of cut-off times; most races have them. For most 50k races, the cutoff time is 8 hours, and it is 12 hours for a 50-mile race. Hundred-mile races have cutoff times of 30 to 48 hours. Ian Torrence, who has run more than 100 ultras and has won first place in 30 of those races, has learned, "One of the big things to remember is to run your own race. It is easy to get caught up in the excitement in the beginning and go too fast. Ultras are not won in the first 15 to 20 miles. After the halfway point, then you can worry about who is in front. If you're running 100 miles, that's about 18 hours. A lot can change within that time, so you have to really listen to your body."

Walking breaks are common in races more than 50 miles. "Walk the uphills, run the downhills" is a familiar mantra among experienced ultrarunners.

One mental strategy used to handle the seemingly overwhelming distance of a 50- or 100-miler is to break the race up into stages. Often runners use an "aid-station-to-aid-station" attitude, running the best possible pace within that distance. Others break the race into thirds.

Pace is an important consideration. A 50-miler takes the average runner 10 hours to complete, which equals a 12-minute mile pace. Tracking your pace on long trail runs will give you a reference point to set your finishing time goals. "The most successful runners must be adaptable, and ready to change with conditions," Kevin Setnes cautions, "Weather can change, even as much as 50 degrees in a race, or the body may require a different pace. You have to be aware of that and adapt."

MULTIDAY EVENTS

In addition to single-day ultras, there are multiday runs, races, and tours to further explore trail running. Multiday events take careful planning for gear, clothing, food, and hydration. Events vary as to the level of assistance provided. Training for a multiday event should include back-to-back long runs, which will prepare your mind and body to run on tired legs and in an exhausted state.

The thrill of adventure running has changed the way many use vacation time. Sedentary trips to the beach for sunbathing are being replaced by exciting trips to exotic lands spent running through ancient ruins and villages. These trips give the trail runner an opportunity to run in other parts of the world, see varied terrain, and meet new people while challenging the mind and body. Trips such as these are memorable.

In the last 10 years, the popularity of adventure tours has grown dramatically. Devy Reinstein, owner of Andes Adven-

tures, has seen his running trips increase from two a year five years ago to fourteen a year. Although trekking trips have been around for a long time, running tours have only recently become popular. Running trips, such as those in Peru or Patagonia, give the runner the luxury of letting someone else handle all the details of food, lodging, and transportation while experiencing the excitement of daily runs through ancient ruins, mountain passes, meadows, and more. Combine that with the chance to learn about other cultures and travel with fellow runners and you have created a very memorable vacation.

SPECIAL CONCERNS FOR ULTRARUNNERS

RECOVERY AND NUTRITION

Recovery from ultras is influenced by age, effort level, genetics, and training base, just as it is for races of shorter distances. However, 50- and 100-mile races and training runs over 25 miles put additional stress not only on the muscle fibers and connective tissues, but also on the endocrine system. The endocrine system produces hormones that govern bodily activities such as water and mineral regulation, sleep, growth, stress, and hunger. It repairs more slowly than muscle fibers and connective tissues, so it is important to allow additional time for the endocrine system to recover.

Most ultrarunners find that recovery slows as they age. Also, if you run an ultra at maximum effort, you place more stresses on your body, which needs more time to repair itself. This applies to your training base as well. The more thoroughly you have prepared for an ultra, the less stress you will place on your body during the race, thus enabling faster recovery. This does not mean that more miles equals better fitness. As mentioned earlier, bodies have different mileage levels they can handle before breaking down. The key is to train at a level that optimizes fitness, while reducing the chance for injury. Understanding that level means listening very closely to your own body and responding appropriately if you are undertraining or overtraining. If you are just beginning to do ultras, keep a long-term approach in mind. It is easy to get caught up in entering multiple events once you reach a certain fitness level and feel the exhilaration of completing a 50- or 100-miler.

The appropriate recovery measures help prevent long-term injuries. According to Karl King, developer of the SUCCEED! supplements, "The first week is for recovery from DOMS [delayed-onset muscle soreness]. Weeks two through four are for healing damaged muscle fibers. By the end of four weeks, most of the muscle fibers are completely healed. Weeks five through six are needed for the complete healing of the endocrine system. It is not unusual for a runner to go out at four weeks and feel fine for many miles, only to crash late in a run when the endocrine system cannot respond to the stress."

Proper hydration, nutrition, and rest are critical during recovery. After an ultra, consume additional protein to promote muscle repair.

Taking the time needed to properly train, taper, and recover from an event allows an ultrarunner to compete in about three events per year, although some runners find that one event a year is all their bodies can handle. There are exceptions. In fact, many ultrarunners compete as often as every month. Listening to your own body and understanding its limitations is essential to attain longevity in running.

FOOT CARE

Ultrarunning places additional stresses on the feet and necessitates careful preventive measures. Blisters are the most common problem, and they are easily prevented. Blisters occur only in the presence of three elements: heat, moisture, and friction. Eliminate one element and you have prevented a blister.

Using powders or antiperspirants on the feet, wearing socks with wicking properties, or wearing double-layered socks can reduce friction and moisture. Lubricants are also used to reduce friction, but they are effective only for about an hour and then must be reapplied. For foot care on the trail, take along the following items in addition to your regular first-aid kit:

- Foot powder in a 35-mm film canister
- Toenail clippers
- Emery boards
- Antiseptic ointment

- Alcohol wipe packets
- Needle and matches for blister puncturing
- Lubricant in a small container
- Duct or other wrapping tape and scissors
- Pieces of moleskin or toilet tissue for blisters

ADVENTURE AND EXPEDITION RACING: THE ULTIMATE CHALLENGE

Adventure races and expedition races are an exciting challenge for an accomplished trail runner who wants to incorporate other skills and compete in a team environment.

Adventure races are mostly races lasting 24 hours or less and do not involve navigational skills. These races usually involve mountain biking, river kayaking, and whitewater rafting in addition to trail running.

Expedition races typically are 6- to 12-day events. Expedition races often include horseback riding, ocean kayaking, mountain climbing, and expert navigational skills; teams must cover varying terrain such as mountains, deserts, jungles, swamps, ocean, and raging rivers. In expedition racing, the course to the finish is not clear-cut. Between checkpoints, teams may select what they believe is the fastest route. Unpredictable factors such as weather often determine which route is the best.

Both adventure and expedition races involve teams of three to five people who must pass various checkpoints and reach the finish line as soon as possible. Teams are required to finish together, using whatever methods of transportation possible. In some races, assistants wait at checkpoints with prepared food, clothing, and equipment. In other races, team members must be completely self-sufficient.

Trail runners have an advantage in both adventure and expedition races because most of the course is off road. Many trail runners attain mountain-biking skills readily because they are already familiar with negotiating uneven trail surfaces such as rocks and roots. Trail running also provides many opportunities to practice navigation.

Multisport event participants often compete with a sense of camaraderie and cooperation not found in any other sport. It is common for opposing teams to assist one another if a team or one of its members is injured, lost, or unable to continue. This may be because of the potential dangers adventure racers face on the course.

Multisport events started early in the 1980s in New Zealand, with the idea of a multiday event coming to life in 1983 with the Coast to Coast. Some of the most renowned events are the Raid Gauloises, the Southern Traverse, and probably the most famous, with more than 1 billion households receiving its TV show annually, the Eco-Challenge. In Derek Paterson's *Adventure Racing: Guide to Survival,* Mark Burnett, founder of the Eco-Challenge, describes expedition racing as "a non-stop, non-motorized, team-based expedition with a stopwatch." He defines the Eco-Challenge as expedition racing to differentiate multiday events from single-day events. Burnett has added an additional challenge to adventure racing: requiring teams to have their own gear and food prepared at the checkpoints in advance, thus doing away with assistants. His experience with the Eco-Challenge and other events is that teamwork is the single most important attribute for success.

The races are held in locations such as Patagonia, New Zealand, Borneo, Morocco, and Utah. Participants often get only 4 to 8 hours of sleep during a 7-day event. Single-day adventure races, such as the Hi-Tec, which takes 3 to 6 hours to complete, and the FogDog, a 24-hour event, mimic the challenges of a multiday event, often including mental and logic challenges.

One of the main differences between both adventure and expedition racing and trail racing is that the former involve working well with a team. According to Cathy Sassin, one of the world's top adventure racers, "It's about knowing that everyone is committed to achieving the goal. That commitment is more important than their physical skills. I've seen people who have this relentless attitude that they're just going to keep trying, no matter what. They constantly work together, and have a positive attitude. They often do better than the team who is better physically qualified, but doesn't have that sense of commitment." Team member Rebecca Rusch, a finisher of the 1999 Patagonia Eco-Challenge, says that the primary reason most teams drop out is not physical problems but personality conflicts or attitude problems.

GETTING STARTED

Breaking into adventure or expedition racing, like running ultras, takes a serious, focused time and energy commitment. Most high-level competitors have a professional background in at least one of the sports involved and have strong skills in all the others. According to Ian Adamson, one of the world's top adventure racers, you have to be a good generalist. There are still many who compete just to finish, which is an accomplishment to be celebrated in itself. Andy Petranek, professional adventure racer, comments that the most successful racers "have the ability to deny acknowledging the bodily pain, and keep moving forward despite serious exhaustion."

You should first determine which skills you need to acquire; mountain biking, kayaking, rafting, swimming, rappelling, and snowshoeing are all potential skills you may need. You should join any available clubs organized around those sports to learn the necessary skills. Navigating and orienteering courses also are available.

Although book knowledge is useful, practicing these skills is critical to your success. Good navigational and map-reading skills are essential. Slow kayaking or mountain biking may delay your team by 30 minutes, but poor navigational skills can cost you hours or days. Mark Burnett suggests, "Start by adventure racing in the short, easier races and work toward the expedition race level.

The ultimate goal should be 8 to 11 days in the wilds of nature with your three teammates against nature in the raw. It is then you know you are alive."

SKILLS NEEDED

With the increasing popularity of multi-sport events, many adventure racing schools have opened throughout the United States. Two and 3-day clinics offer introductory or advanced-level skills and sometimes conclude with a minicourse in which participants practice their skills. Before enrolling, consider the experience and résumés of the instructors and the content of the course. Talk to previous clients to determine whether the course is for you.

In addition to joining an orienteering club, there are other ways to improve your navigation skills. Each time you run, take a map and mark a few points. On the run, go from point to point and identify each point as you reach it. Practice navigating at night or in rainy or foggy conditions, when you cannot use the sun as a directional guide. Practice going cross-country, off trails, or in dense brush, as long as this does not threaten the environment. Practice in a class or group or with a coach or other experienced person.

All water sports help build upper-body strength; distance runners usually have more strength in their lower bodies. Upper-body strength is essential in a multisport event. You are always pulling yourself up out of a ravine or onto a boat or lifting your bike. Proper paddling technique conserves energy and can prevent paddling injuries such as tendonitis. In addition to technique, practice in varied conditions. Kayaking on a quiet, gentle river is very different from rafting in class IV rapids or kayaking on the open ocean. The more you duplicate possible race conditions, the greater your chances of success.

Many trail runners limit their cross-training to mountain biking under normal conditions, but you should practice some additional skills to adapt to adventure and expedition racing. First, ride with a heavy pack. The extra weight changes your center of gravity, thus changing the way you handle hills and braking. Long uphill rides help develop strong quadriceps muscles, and long downhills develop agility and balance. Practicing speed on downhills also increases your confidence. Practice biking at night using a headlamp. Some bike clubs sponsor nighttime rides.

In addition to navigation and biking skills, climbing knowledge is needed. The popularity of climbing walls at many gyms has made a basic understanding of this sport accessible. However, practicing in a gym is very different from climbing outdoors. You should practice these skills outdoors with a reliable, licensed guide or in an approved class and become familiar with the equipment used in climbing. In addition, weather conditions such as heavy winds, ice, or snow and climbing at night can dramatically affect the degree of difficulty in negotiating a mountain.

KEYS TO SUCCESS

Successful adventure and expedition racing means moving forward in the face of exhaustion, stress, sleep deprivation, hunger, thirst, fear, and pain. It also takes excellent teamwork and communication. Cathy Sassin comments, "In these races, you start feeling for, with, and from other people. If someone usually talks a lot and they get quiet, or their gait changes, or they're shifting around their pack, or other subtle changes, you have to be aware of those and take care of them before they become an issue. You have to be rid of your ego. Everyone is doing the best they can. We all help each other. You have to get past worrying about if you're carrying your own load or how you compare to others."

Ian Adamson, who holds world records in many adventure sports, notes, "Great teamwork will keep a team moving a lot faster than the slowest member alone. Successful teamwork dictates that the weight is unevenly distributed so that everyone moves at the same speed with the same effort."

Beginners should train together, if possible, and get a clear understanding of each other's strengths and weaknesses. Everyone may have a great attitude when conditions are comfortable, but moderately stressful situations more closely reproduce the actual race environment.

Managing sleep deprivation is another obstacle. Sassin adds, "Competitive teams don't sleep at all the first night. The second night, if you're at altitude, you have to sleep a little for the body to recover. If you are at low elevation, it is not necessary to sleep.

One rule is that if two of the four or five people are okay, and two are really tired, then you can pull the tired people through. But if it is more than two, it is wasted energy to try to move forward. Or, if the navigator cannot function well, you have to rest. We find that 10 to 15 minutes will buy us two to three hours. Sleeping an hour will buy you about six hours. When the sun comes up, it always provides energy. Usually 11 P.M. to midnight, and 4 to 5 A.M. is when the body is most sleepy. But if you push through that low point, it will go away. Your body just cycles through it. Most people don't realize that." She also comments that beginners can sleep 2 to 4 hours a night and still make the cutoff times.

SUPPORT CREWS AND PACERS

Volunteering at races, working on a support crew, and working as a pacer are all excellent ways to increase your knowledge of ultrarunning. Pacing and crewing allow you to learn details of a particular event and gain valuable insight. Crewing and pacing also are rewarding ways to be part of a team, even if you are not ready to compete. The success of an ultrarunner or adventure racer depends largely on the crew's ability to communicate and to anticipate what is needed in an organized way.

Support crews are the team members who provide assistance at aid stations. They drive from checkpoint to checkpoint, preparing clothing, gear, food, water, motivation, first aid, or whatever else is needed at the time. There may be only one member, or there may be several.

Pacers run with the runner for varying legs, such as 25- or 40-mile distances, usually in the second half of a race. Pacers may take turns and usually are part of the support crew.

All support team members must become very familiar with the course and plan strategy with the runner before the race. The following are some key suggestions for assisting a runner as part of a crew:

- Study the course; run parts of it. Study aid station locations and course markings. Read the entrants' handbook and study the rules and other pertinent information.

- Organize the vehicle so that it makes sense to the athlete and everyone working out of it. Keep it clean and organized throughout the race so time is not wasted locating items.

- Schedule crew rest breaks. At least one crew member must be alert and well rested. If there are only two crew members, plan to get little sleep. Crews should have a portable alarm clock.

- Find out what each runner wants at each aid station and when he or she expects to be at each station. Arrive at least 45 minutes ahead of schedule and be ready with food, gear, or water. Stay aware of what is available for the runner.

- Plan how you will get food and water for yourself. Bring enough clothing to stay warm. It is easy for crews to forget about themselves. An ill crew member is useless to the runner.

- Ascertain the crew members' knowledge of blister treatment. Find out how the runner normally prepares his or her feet before the race and how he or she prefers to handle blisters. At least one crew member should be knowledgeable in first aid and foot care.

- At aid stations, have food, water, and gear ready in advance. Urge the runner to eat and drink even if he or she does not want to. Keep bringing water until the runner solidly refuses. Refill water bottles.

- Keep the runner moving. Don't let him or her stop too long.

Pacers offer motivation and companionship while keeping the runner on the right course. Communication before the race is essential because in the latter stages of a race, a runner may not be thinking clearly or able to make coherent decisions. You should find out whether the runner wants you to run in front or behind, what he or she wants you to carry, whether he or she prefers conversation or quiet, and whether there are points in the race when you should push him or her to go faster. You should also be well aware of the rules of a race; most races have a "no-muling" rule, which means you are not supposed to carry the runner's clothes, food, water, or spare batteries. Some races allow the pacer to carry emergency supplies such as a first-aid kit, blister kit, or extra food and drink. The following are some helpful suggestions for pacers:

- Bring plenty of batteries, bulbs, and flashlights for the nighttime portion. Before the race, practice changing bulbs and batteries in the dark.

- Monitor the pace carefully and keep the runner moving forward as close to the desired pace as possible. Let the runner walk for a short period, if necessary, but remind him or her of the goal. If you run slightly in front of the runner, he or she will be motivated to keep up. If you are going uphill, ask whether he or she wants to be pushed. If so, go in front of the runner.

- If the course becomes technical, go ahead and scout the best route. Scout ahead for slippery or other tricky portions of the trail.

- On turns, allow the runner to be on the inside.

- Be positive and motivating. The runner may not have the energy to respond, but he or she may appreciate the encouragement.

- During the night or in the latter portions of the race, the runner may experience low points and want to quit. He or she may become tired or cranky. Talk about the finish line, and help the runner envision crossing it. When the sun comes up, he or she will get a boost of energy. Unless the runner is seriously injured, keep him or her moving forward, even if that means taking short walking breaks.

- Force the runner to drink and eat. He or she may not be in a sharp mental state and may easily forget. Many DNFs (did not finishes) are caused by dehydration or a lack of food.

- Bring a camera and document the event, but do not take flash pictures at night because this will impair the runner's night vision.

- Most importantly, be sensitive to what the runner needs and look out for his or her best interests.

Appendix A: Responsible Trail Running Guidelines

These guidelines were written by Tom Sobal and first appeared in *Trail Times,* the newsletter published by the All American Trail Running Association (AATRA), Volume 3, No. 11. Tom Sobal and the AATRA have graciously allowed them to be reprinted here with minor modifications by the authors.

1. Stay on marked and existing trails. Stay off closed trails and obey all posted regulations.
2. Do not cut switchbacks.
3. Go through puddles, not around them.
4. Climb under or jump over fallen trees instead of going around them.
5. When multiple trails exist, run on the one that is the most worn.
6. Do not litter, leave no trace, and pack everything out that you have packed in.
7. Use minimum impact techniques to dispose of human waste.
8. Leave what you find—take only photographs.
9. Close all gates that you open.
10. Respect private property. Get permission first to go on private land.
11. Do not run on muddy or very dusty trails. Pick another route so that you do not damage the trail and cause unnecessary erosion.
12. Avoid startling other runners and trail users when passing from behind by calling out "hello" well in advance.
13. Be ready to yield to other trail users (cyclists, hikers, and horses).
14. Uphill runners yield to downhill runners.
15. Know the area where you plan to run and let at least one other person know where you are going.

16. Dress for the conditions, both existing and potential.
17. Carry plenty of water.
18. Know your limits.
19. Stop to help others in need even while racing. Sacrifice your event to aid other trail users who might be in trouble.
20. Volunteer at trail races before, after, and during the event.
21. Volunteer for, support, and encourage others to participate in trail maintenance days.
22. Do not disturb or harass wildlife or livestock.

Appendix B: Resources

Adventure and Expedition Racing Websites

Andes Adventures
www.andesadventures.com

Adventure Racing Association (ARA)
email list at
mailto:listserve@adventureracing.org

Adventure Training
www.adventuretrain.com

Cal Eco Series
www.csmevents.com

Eco Challenge
www.ecochallenge.com

Explore.com
*www.explore.com/endurance/
contents.cfm*

Odyssey Adventure Racing
email list at *mailto:oarinfo@aol.com*

Southern California Adventure Racing
Buddies
www.scarabs.homestead.com

Animal and Plant Safety

Alaska Science Forum (article on pepper
spray)
*www.gi.alaska.edu/ScienceForum/
ASF12/1245.html*

GORP.com (article on preventing snakebites)
*www.gorp.com/gorp/health/
snakefaq14.htm*

Knowledgehound: The How-To Hunter
(articles on wildlife protection and
safety)
*www.knowledgehound.com/topics/
wildlife.htm*

Wildlife Watcher (news and information)
www.wildlifewatcher.com/safe.phtml

Equipment

Adventure Network
www.adventurenetwork.com

Boulder Bars
www.boulderbar.com
(858) 274-1049

Clif Bars
www.clifbar.com
(800) 884-5254

Fog Dog Sports
www.fogdog.com

Gu Products
www.gusports.com
(800) 400-1995

Hammer Nutrition
www.hammergel.com
(800)336-1977

Mountain Hardwear
www.mountainhardwear.com
(510) 559-6700

Pearl Izumi Clothing
www.pearlizumi.com
(800) 328-8488

Polar Heart Rate Monitors
www.polarheartratemonitors.com
(888) 477-6527

Roadrunner Sports Catalog
www.roadrunnersports.com
(800) 636-3560

Smartwool Socks
www.smartwool.com
(800) 550-WOOL

Sporthill Clothing
www.sporthill.com
(800) 622-8444

SUCCEED! Products
www.ultrafit-endurance.com
(888) 838-2802

Sun Precautions
www.sunprecautions.com
(800) 882-7860

Suunto Watches
www.suuntousa.com
(800) 543-9124

Tecnu Skin Protector and Cleanser
www.teclabsinc.com
(800) ITCHING

Timberland Products
www.mountainathletics.com

Ultima Replenisher
www.ultimareplenisher.com
(888) 663-8584

First-Aid Kits
Brave Soldier
www.bravesoldier.com

Sawyer Products
www.sawyerproducts.com
(800) 940-4464

General Travel, Fitness, and Running
GORP.com (recreation and travel site)
www.gorp.com

Mountain Running (trail information)
www.mountainrunning.com

Oceans of Energy (spiritually oriented
information on sports, fitness, and
yoga)
www.oceansofenergy.com

Run-Down (all-purpose runners' site)
www.run-down.com

Runner's World on women's running
www.womens-running.com

Trails.com (trail information)
www.trails.com

Hydration Systems
Blackburn
www.blackburndesign.com

Camelbak
www.camelbak.com
(800)767-8725
Ultimate Directions
www.ultdir.com
(800) 426 7229

Medical Kit Suppliers

Adventure Medical Kits
(800) 324-3517
Atwater Carey
(800) 359-1646
Outdoor Research
(800) 421-2421
Sawyer
(800) 356-7811

Navigation

Kjetil Kjernsmo's illustrated guide on
how to use a compass
www.astro.uio.no/~kjetikj/compass/
U.S. Orienteering Federation
www.us.orienteering.org

Nutrition

American Council on Fitness
www.acefitness.org
American Heart Association
www.americanheart.org
National Association for Health and
Fitness
www.physicalfitness.org
The Physician and Sportsmedicine
Online
www.physsportsmed.com
Running Research News
www.rrnews.com

U.S. Department of Agriculture
www.usda.gov

Publications

Runner's World
www.runnersworld.com
Running Times
www.runningtimes.com
Trail Runner Magazine
www.trailrunnermag.com
Ultrarunning Magazine
www.ultrarunning.com

Race Websites

www.active.com
www.badwaterultra.com
www.deadseamarathon.com
www.leadvilletrail100.com
www.runningonthesun.com

Shoes

Adidas
www.adidas.com
Asics
www.asicstiger.com
Brooks
www.brookssports.com
Fila
www.fila.com
Montrail
www.montrail.com
New Balance
www.newbalance.com
Nike
www.nike.com
The North Face
www.thenorthface.com

Reebok
www.reebok.com
Salomon
www.salomonsports.com
Saucony
www.saucony.com
Teva
www.teva.com

Trail Running Organizations

All American Trail Running Association
(AATRA)
P.O. Box 9175
Colorado Springs, CO 89932
(719) 570-9795
www.trailrunner.com
Road Runners Club of America (RRCA)
1150 South Washington Ave., Suite 250
Alexandria, VA 22314
(703) 836-0558
www.rrca.org

Ultrarunning Websites

www.fred.net/ultrunr
www.ultrarunner.net
www.ultrarunning.com

Weather and Government Organizations

Bureau of Land Management
www.blm.gov
National Park Service
www.nps.gov
National Weather Service
www.nws.noaa.gov
U.S. Air Quality
www.epa.gov/airnow
U.S. Forest Service
www.fs.fed.us

Appendix C: Equipment Lists for Short, Medium, and Longer Runs

Specific trail conditions may necessitate certain items, and how much you carry is largely a matter of personal preference. Some runners want to carry as little as possible; for others, thorough preparation is the priority. These lists are intended for use as guidelines only; equipment needs vary according to weather conditions and course difficulty. Your preferences will develop as you become more experienced.

Short Run (less than 1 hour)

30 to 80 ounces of water
First-aid kit
One or two snack items
Sunscreen
Whistle
Watch
Course map and compass
Sunglasses and hat

Medium Run (1 to 2 hours)

50 to 100 ounces of water
First-aid kit
Two or three snack items
Sunscreen
Whistle
Watch
Course map and compass
Sunglasses and hat

Long Run (more than 2 hours)

80 to 120 ounces of water mixed with an
    electrolyte replacement
First-aid kit (more complete than on
    shorter runs)
Three or four snack items
Sunscreen
Whistle
Watch
Course map and compass
Sunglasses and hat

Pain reliever such as ibuprofen, acetaminophen, or aspirin

Very Long Run (more than 4 hours)

Everything listed for shorter runs and more, depending on conditions.
Water filtration system
Snack items that contain protein
Dry socks
Windbreaker or waterproof jacket
Space blanket
Matches
GPS
Flashlight
Knife
Additional first-aid supplies such as gauze pads, tape, elastic bandage, and signal mirror.

Items to Keep in your Car

Extra water to drink or use to rinse off
Clean shirt
Clean pair of socks
Sandals or shoes
Brush to clean off your shoes
Extra food
Towel
Bag to hold dirty items
Cell phone to notify friends or family that you are safely off the trail
Complete first-aid kit
Ice (in case you sustain an injury and cannot find immediate medical treatment)

Bibliography

American College of Sports Medicine. "Positions on Osteoporosis and Exercise." *Medicine and Science in Sports and Exercise* 27 (1995): I–IV.

Armstrong, Lawrence E. *Performing in Extreme Environments.* Champaign, Ill.: Human Kinetics, 2000.

Burns, Bob and Mike Burns. *Wilderness Navigation, Finding Your Way Using Map, Compass, Altimeter, & GPS.* Seattle: The Mountaineers Books, 1999.

Christian, Janet L. and Janet L. Greger. *Nutrition for Living.* Redwood City, Calif.: Benjamin/Cummings, 1994.

Coleman, Ellen and Suzanne Nelson Steen. *Ultimate Sports Nutrition,* 2nd ed. Palo Alto, Calif.: Bull Publishing, 2000.

Conroy, B.P. and coauthors. "Bone Mineral Density in Elite Junior Olympic Weightlifters." *Medicine and Science in Sports and Exercise* 25 (1995): 1103–1109.

Ellis, Joe. *Running Injury-Free.* Emmaus, Pa.: Rodale, 1994.

Folsom, A. R. and coauthors. "Physical Activity and Incidence of Coronary Heart Diseases in Middle-Aged Women and Men." *Medicine and Science in Sports and Exercise 29* (1997): 901–909.

Galloway, Jeff. *Galloway's Book on Running.* Bolinas, Calif.: Shelter, 1984.

Glover, Bob and Pete Schuder. *The New Competitive Runner's Handbook.* New York: Penguin, 1988.

Letham, Lawrence. *GPS Made Easy,* 2nd ed. Seattle: The Mountaineers Books, 1998.

McManners, Hugh. *The Backpacker's Handbook.* London: Dorling Kindersley Limited, 1995.

Mensink, G. B. M. and coauthors. "Intensity, Duration and Frequency of Physical Activity and Coronary Risk Heart Factors." *Medicine and Science in Sports and Science* 29 (1997): 1192–1198.

Miller, G. Tyler. *Environmental Science: an Introduction.* 2nd ed. Belmont, Calif.: Wadsworth, 1988.

Nieman, D.C. "Exercise, Upper Respiratory Tract Infection, and the Immune System." *Medicine and Science in Sports and Exercise* 26 (1994): 128–139.

Ogg, Barb. *Itchy Chiggers!* Lincoln: University of Nebraska Cooperative Extension, 1996.

Paterson, Derek. *Adventure Racing: Guide to Survival.* Sporting Endeavours, 1999.

Pavelka, Ed, ed. *Bicycling Magazine's Nutrition for Peak Performance.* Emmaus, Pa.: Rodale, 2000.

Samuelson, Joan. *Running for Women.* Emmaus, Pa.: Rodale, 1995.

Schad, Jerry. *Afoot and Afield in Los Angeles County.* Berkeley, Calif.: Wilderness Press, 1991.

Schad, Jerry, and David Moser, eds. *Wilderness Basics: The Complete Handbook for Hikers and Backpackers,* 2nd ed. Seattle: The Mountaineers Books, 1992.

Swartz, Stan, Jim Wolff, and Samir Shahin. *50 Trail Runs in Southern California.* Seattle: The Mountaineers Books, 2000.

Teegarden, D. and coauthors. "Previous Physical Activity Relates to Bone Mineral Measures in Young Women." *Medicine and Science in Sports and Exercise* 28 (1996): 105–113.

Vonhof, John. *Fixing Your Feet, Prevention and Treatments for Athletes,* 2nd ed. Fremont, Calif.: Foothill, 2000.

Wilmore, J.H. "Increasing Physical Activity; Alterations in Body Mass and Composition." *American Journal of Clinical Nutrition* 63 (1996): 456S–460S.

Index

About the Authors

Paula Petrella

Kirsten Poulin is an accomplished trail runner and recently retired business owner. She has been running trails for eight years and is a regular participant in running events from 10 to 50 kilometers. As a member of the Trail Runners Club, she has traveled to runs including an annual 40-mile Grand Canyon rim-to-rim trip and multiday runs such as an 85-mile run in the Peruvian Andes and a 180-mile run in the wilds of Patagonia. These experiences gave her the opportunity to hear and share in many stories of inspiration, accomplishment, and overcoming obstacles.

She has taught young people in areas of self-confidence, personal development, and basic nutrition and has coached beginning runners. She lives in southern California with her husband, a television-series writer.

Stan Swartz founded the Trail Runners Club in 1988 and has been its director since its inception. He also cofounded the Pacific Palisades Pacers Running Club before turning to trail running. He has organized many off-road running events and was invited to be an advisor to the All American Trail Running Association. Along with Jim Wolff and Samir Shahin, M.D., he coauthored *50 Trail Runs in Southern California,* published in early 2000 by The Mountaineers Books.

Christina Flaxel, M.D., is an ophthalmologist and serious runner. Over the past twenty-five years she has completed seven marathons and many trail races. She is also an avid triathlete and mountain biker. She is an active member of the Loma Linda Lopers Running Club and the Trail Runners Club of Santa Monica. She is assistant clinical professor at the University of Southern California, Keck School of Medicine, Los Angeles.

THE MOUNTAINEERS, founded in 1906, is a nonprofit outdoor activity and conservation club, whose mission is "to explore, study, preserve, and enjoy the natural beauty of the outdoors . . . ." Based in Seattle, Washington, the club is now the third-largest such organization in the United States, with 15,000 members and five branches throughout Washington State.

The Mountaineers sponsors both classes and year-round outdoor activities in the Pacific Northwest, which include hiking, mountain climbing, ski-touring, snowshoeing, bicycling, camping, kayaking and canoeing, nature study, sailing, and adventure travel. The club's conservation division supports environmental causes through educational activities, sponsoring legislation, and presenting informational programs. All club activities are led by skilled, experienced volunteers, who are dedicated to promoting safe and responsible enjoyment and preservation of the outdoors.

If you would like to participate in these organized outdoor activities or the club's programs, consider a membership in The Mountaineers. For information and an application, write or call The Mountaineers, Club Headquarters, 300 Third Avenue West, Seattle, WA 98119; 206-284-6310.

The Mountaineers Books, an active, nonprofit publishing program of the club, produces guidebooks, instructional texts, historical works, natural history guides, and works on environmental conservation. All books produced by The Mountaineers Books fulfill the club's mission.

Send or call for our catalog of more than 500 outdoor titles:

The Mountaineers Books
1001 SW Klickitat Way, Suite 201
Seattle, WA 98134
800-553-4453
mbooks@mountaineersbooks.org
www.mountaineersbooks.org

TRAIL RUNNER, *The Magazine of Running Adventure,* is the first nationally distributed, full-color magazine devoted to off-road running. It covers all aspects of trail running, from leisurely fitness runs to grueling, high-altitude ultra-marathons, as well as snowshoeing, adventure racing, and orienteering. Our mission is to inform, entertain, and invigorate trail runners of all abilities with interesting news coverage, useful training and nutritional advice, critical product reviews, and inspirational features. Trail Runner is published in Boulder, Colorado, by North South Publications, which also produces the award-winning climbing magazine *Rock & Ice.*

To subscribe, call toll-free 877-762-5423 or visit us online at *www.trailrunnermag.com.*

the magazine of running adventure